YORK NOT]

General Editors: Professor
of Stirling) & Professor Su
University of Beirut)

John Webster

THE WHITE DEVIL

Notes by Michael Jardine

MA (NEWCASTLE) PH D (SHAKESPEARE INSTITUTE, BIRMINGHAM)
Lecturer in English, King Alfred's College, Winchester

**LONGMAN
YORK PRESS**

YORK PRESS
Immeuble Esseily, Place Riad Solh, Beirut.

LONGMAN GROUP UK LIMITED
Burnt Mill,
Harlow, Essex

First published 1982
Second impression 1986

ISBN 0-582-78264-3

Produced by Longman Group (FE) Ltd
Printed in Hong Kong

Contents

Part 1

Introduction

The life of John Webster

In a poem published in 1624 Webster reveals that he was 'born free' of the Merchant Taylor's Company. As a builder of coaches his father, another John Webster, belonged to that Company, and when he died in about 1615 his eldest son John inherited a flourishing business, so that, unlike most of the hired writers who provided play-scripts for the theatres, Webster (at least for the last twenty years of his life) had a private source of income. This might explain why he wrote little for the stage after his two masterpieces, *The White Devil* (1612) and *The Duchess of Malfi* (1614). His involvement in commerce is referred to mockingly by one Henry Fitzjeffrey, who, in a poem published in 1617, refers to 'crabbed Websterio,/The playwright-cartwright.' He also reveals Webster's extreme slowness in writing his plays: 'See how he draws his mouth awry of late,/How he scrubs, wrings his wrists, scratches his pate./A midwife, help!'

Webster must have been born by 1580 as he was collaborating in the writing of plays by 1602. He married a sixteen-year-old named Sara Peniall, daughter of a saddler, in about 1605 and she gave birth to the first of numerous children in 1606. Webster's education would have begun at the Merchant Taylor's School, which had been built up by a famous educationalist, Richard Mulcaster, and had a high reputation. Here the teaching of languages, classical and modern, was central to the curriculum, but the schooling was broad enough to include music, the performing of plays, and all sorts of physical exercise. The evidence suggests that Webster went on to study law, being admitted to the New Inn in 1598. This helps to account for the numerous legal references and trial scenes in his work.

Between 1602 and the publication of *The White Devil* in 1612 Webster seems to have preferred to collaborate in writing and adapting plays. Such a long apprenticeship suggests that he was not an independently inventive dramatist, and, as Fitzjeffrey indicates, he wrote slowly and was heavily dependent on the works of others and on current literary trends. His reputation was enhanced by publication of *The White Devil*, and we find him asserting his status as a poet by publishing an elegy on the death of Prince Henry, heir to the throne, who, like Brachiano in *The White Devil*, died in the lists. After *The Duchess of Malfi*, considered by many to be his greatest play, Webster participated in the general decline in theatrical standards marked by the departure of Shakespeare, who died in 1616. His tragi-comedy, *The Devil's Law Case*, performed shortly after 1616, lacks the power and authority of his two great tragedies. After this he returned to collaborative work, possibly a sign of a loss in artistic confidence, or perhaps because of his commitments to the business inherited from his father. One biographer has argued that Webster's dramatic activity was governed by his wish to present material to the Lord Mayor of London if he were a Merchant Taylor, and indeed several known dates of the first performance or publication of his plays do coincide with years when the Lord Mayor was a Merchant Taylor; for example, *The White Devil* was first performed when the Merchant Taylor Sir John Swinnerton became Lord Mayor.* It is, however, hard to explain on this basis why he later chose to join forces with three other dramatists to take advantage of two recent scandals – a matricide and a forced marriage – to cobble together a play, now lost, entitled *The Late Murder of the Son upon the Mother, or Keep the Widow Waking*, a work hardly worthy of a Lord Mayor. This noticeable decline in standards endorses J. R. Brown's observation that 'the achievements of 1612–14 were not only hardly won, but also precariously won'.† Webster is thought to have died between 1628 and 1634.

The theatre in Webster's time

We can get an insight into the state of the theatre in early seventeenth-century England from Webster's preface to *The White Devil*. In it he appears as an intellectual alienated from and contemptuous of the popular audience and the large, public theatres of the time. He complains that his tragedy was not well received,

> since it was acted, in so dull a time of winter, presented in so open and black a theatre, that it wanted (that which is the only grace and setting out of a true tragedy) a full and understanding auditory: and that since that time I have noted, most of the people that come to that playhouse, resemble those ignorant asses (who visiting stationers' shops, their use is not to inquire for good books, but new books.)

The playhouse referred to, the Red Bull, was probably capable of holding two to three thousand people, but it attracted a notoriously unsophisticated audience, being 'the subject of more sneers than any other playhouse of the time'.‡ Webster appears to have completely

*M. C. Bradbrook: *John Webster Citizen and Dramatist*, Weidenfeld and Nicolson, London, 1980, p. 141.
†J. R. Brown (ed.): *The White Devil*, Manchester University Press, 1979, p. xxvi.
‡G. E. Bentley: *The Jacobean and Caroline Stage*, (7 vols), Clarendon Press, Oxford, 1941–68, vi, p. 238.

miscalculated the taste of the Red Bull clientele, offering ambitious and complex drama where only clowning, spectacle, and vulgar stage effects were expected.

The most stimulating aspect of the earlier, Elizabethan, playhouses (the first permanent, purpose-built one was the Theatre, constructed in 1575–6) was their ability to attract the whole range of society, from lords to labourers. Webster appears to be writing for such a mixed audience, as *The White Devil* combines spectacular with subtle effects; but the time of such integration was passing, or had passed, and with it the golden age of English drama was coming to a close. It seems that since the turn of the seventeenth century there had been a growing tendency among playwrights to cater for either lords or labourers, not both, and in this respect Webster's play is rather old-fashioned. This change was sparked off by the success of children's companies whose performances in private, indoor theatres were designed for an upper-class audience. The adult companies were forced to compete for this lucrative market, and fewer plays were written with a broad appeal. Webster, however, learned from his misjudgment in selling *The White Devil* to the Queen's Men to be acted at the Red Bull, as his next play went to Shakespeare's company, the King's Men – probably to be played at their indoor theatre with artificial lighting, the Blackfriars.

With artificial lighting in a small hall the dramatist could depend on the audience observing more subtle effects, but public theatres such as the Red Bull were 'open' and could be 'black' when clouds obscured the sun, as Webster's preface complains. Noblemen paid extra for seats actually on the playing area, which was a raised platform projecting into an open yard and backing on to the 'tiring house' where the actors changed. The poorer spectators, who were called 'groundlings', stood in the uncovered yard and were surrounded by tiers of covered galleries from which the better-off looked down on the stage. This platform stage was raised about five feet from the ground and was probably about twenty-seven feet deep and forty-three feet wide, the size of the one at Shakespeare's Globe. A trap-door led to a space beneath, where large stage properties, such as the vaulting horse used in Camillo's murder, could be stored. At the back of the stage were doors, for access to and from the tiring house, and a balcony, which could be used as a playing area. The balcony and part of the rear stage could be curtained off to allow 'discoveries' to be made (such as the murder of Isabella). Two pillars held a roof over the stage (Flamineo is bound to one of them in V.6.183) and there was a mechanical device for ascent and descent. The roof was decorated underneath to represent the heavens: thus the actor walked on the stage (earth) with hell (under the playing area) and heaven (overhead) as ever-present alternatives.

The most vital characteristic of the Elizabethan stage, however, was its neutrality of location, which made it easily and infinitely adaptable. Webster makes full use of this flexibility with rapid changes of location. To an extent the highly imaginative and persuasive blank verse compensated for the lack of scenic background, but the audience also expected and received a good deal of visual splendour, particularly in the costumes on which vast amounts were spent. Plays commonly gave opportunities for expert swordfights, acrobatics, dancing, music, battles, and processions. In *The White Devil* such set pieces as the trial scene and the papal election show Webster's awareness of the value of spectacle, just as the mock-death of Flamineo shows his mastery of dramatic stage effects.

Historical background

In 1603 the reign of Elizabeth I ended and James I succeeded to the throne. By 1611 when *The White Devil* was published it was becoming apparent that James was not coping well with the many problems he faced, both inherited and self-induced. By not extending toleration to dissenting religious groups, he multiplied his enemies (in 1605 there was a Catholic plot, the Gunpowder Plot, to blow up both the king and Parliament). The measures he took to bypass Parliament (in order to get revenue which they were unwilling to grant him) were also unpopular, particularly the sale of monopolies and titles: the former raised prices and the latter damaged the status of the aristocracy. His foreign policy brought criticism because it was based on peace with the old Catholic enemy, Spain. Catholicism seemed to be favoured at court and this, coupled with a general decline in moral standards there, damaged the king's public image. James's reputation was further damaged, and he alienated powerful noble families, by favouring handsome young men, such as George Villiers, who practically governed the country for eleven years. Unlike Elizabeth he did not lead by example and did not inspire loyalty or trust. Yet he made more extreme claims for the rights of monarchs than did his predecessor, telling Parliament in 1609 that 'Kings are not only God's lieutenants on earth and sit upon God's throne, but even by God Himself they are called gods'. Forty years later his own son, Charles I, showed how far from divinity the royal line had fallen in the eyes of many, when he was executed on the order of Parliament.

Elizabethan to Jacobean: a changing world

There is a line from a poem by John Donne (1571–1631) published in the year before *The White Devil* which is often quoted when historians seek to define the mood of England in the early seventeenth century: 'And new philosophy calls all in doubt'. To understand this 'doubt' as well as the 'new philosophy' it is necessary to know something of the attitudes and ideas that were being doubted – to the extent that by 1625 another major poet, Michael Drayton (1563–1631) was writing, 'Certainly there's scarce one found now knows what to approve or what to disallow'. Such uncertainty would not have been voiced a century before: what happened to bring it about was the gradual disintegration of a social order and a system of knowledge inherited from the medieval period (the fifth to the fifteenth century). These had given man a sense of stability and security, as they offered a conception of society and of man's relation to God which was clear, unchangeable and harmonious.

In theory, society was immobile, each man accepting a fixed place in a hierarchy or series of graded ranks, ranging from gentlemen to common labourers. Its basis was feudal and agricultural, vassals holding land on condition of rendering services and dues to a landowner. The relationship was one of mutual obligation, as the master was supposed to give shelter and protection to his dependants in return for loyalty and obedience. The family unit was a vital element of this social order, with wife and children owing allegiance to the father who held responsibility for their welfare. This orthodox view of the world was a strong support to rulers, as it gave divine authority to the *status quo* and to the theory of the 'divine right' of kings to rule with unquestioning obedience from their subjects. Not only human society but the entire universe and everything in it was conceived in terms of a hierarchy of interdependent parts, aptly called a 'great chain of being'. According to its value and merit each thing, from God at the top to inanimate matter at the bottom, had a fixed place on this 'chain'. Man filled a unique place linking pure spirit (angels) with pure bestiality (animals), and it was believed that his future happiness depended on avoiding sin which related him with beasts (as often happens in *The White Devil*), and gaining salvation through God's grace which would earn him promotion to angelic bliss. The planets and the elements were not only in rank order, but this God-given order was created out of what would otherwise be chaos. In the same way man was conceived as a complete world in miniature. The four warring elements termed 'humours', that is, melancholy, blood, choler and phlegm, could coexist in perfect harmony in a healthy man, or be imbalanced and discordant in a mentally or physically diseased man. Physical disorder reflecting a greater disorder is seen in the work of Webster as in that of Shakespeare, who wrote,

The man that hath no musicke in himself . . .
Is fit for treasons, stratagems and spoiles
(*The Merchant of Venice*, V.1.83–5)

For a number of complex reasons this orthodox system of beliefs, which is so beautifully symmetrical, was undermined; and its collapse when it came was absolute, since to question a part was to doubt the whole. The advance of modern science, one aspect of Donne's 'new philosophy', contributed to the undermining. Copernicus (1473–1543) began by demonstrating the earth to be a minor planet orbiting the sun, thus shattering one of the hierarchical schemes. Galileo (1564–1642) discredited the belief that the universe was made up of the elements of earth, water, fire and air in ascending order.

More damaging was the transition from an agricultural to an industrial society which was taking place, as this put pressure on the old feudal ideals of patronage and service. The growth of competitive commercialism introduced greater ruthlessness into relationships: the labourer could sell his labour to the highest bidder, and the man with capital could invest it with the impersonal object of maximising his profits. There was greater social mobility as a result of greater opportunities to make fortunes, or lose them (as Lodovico does: I.1.13–14). The once-stable landed class was in turmoil as patrimonies changed hands at an alarming rate. This hectic pursuit of wealth and power in an unsettled society forms the background of Webster's tragic vision.

Another major source of disruption was the growing influence of a religious movement known as Puritanism. Like capitalism, it promoted individualism, as it invited each man to work out his path to salvation without regard to an organised church. Defined by one historian as 'a driving enthusiasm for moral improvement in every aspect of life',* it substituted a hierarchy of godliness for the old hierarchy of rank, with the revolutionary effect that a godly subject could be preferred to an ungodly king. Catholics and other less well-known religious groups also dissented from the Established Church, and there was a growing sense of there being no plainly right way to achieve salvation. In this highly religious age, when death was so much closer than for the twentieth-century Englishman, such a consideration was a major contributor to the mood of scepticism which characterises this period. The great tragedies which were written in the first dozen years of the seventeenth century (including four by Shakespeare and two by Webster) are tragedies principally because they are written in full awareness of the glorious potential of the human spirit, which had been at the core of Renaissance humanism, but with this glory enveloped and perhaps extinguished by evil in its most corrupt and disfigured shapes.

*L. Stone: *The Crisis of the English Revolution*, Routledge & Kegan Paul, London, 1972, p. 99.

Melancholy, Machiavelli, and the Jacobean stage

Two related aspects of the disintegration of the humanistic ideal which are of interest in a study of drama of this period, and of Webster in particular, are the fascination firstly with a type of behaviour defined as melancholic, and secondly with a political ideology called machiavellianism. An early Elizabethan definition of excess melancholy is:

> Melancholic Man hath nature of Earth, cold and dry. He is heavy, covetous, backbiter, malicious and slow ... And he loveth black colour.

By the Jacobean period, however, it had become fashionable to be melancholic (see *The White Devil*, III.3.66–97, for evidence of this), as its speculative nature made it the disease of intellectuals. Shakespeare's Hamlet, with his black clothing and bitter railing against humanity, was an early stage example of the melancholic intellectual. Society at this time provided many real examples of disaffected intellectuals (often graduates) unable to find employment suited to their talents and expectations. It is from their ranks, in fact, that most of the playwrights came. They made the educated malcontent into a conventional stage figure, a satirical commentator on a corrupt court from which he is excluded. Webster makes good use of this figure in his tragedies, with Flamineo in *The White Devil* and Bosola in *The Duchess of Malfi*.

These discontented and often desperate characters, cynically indifferent to accepted moral standards, not only stand outside and rail against society but, paradoxically, are ambitious for power within it. This makes them ideal instruments for another favourite stage type of the time, the Machiavel. The Italian statesman and writer Machiavelli (1469–1527) achieved notoriety through such statements as, 'Men do not work in the direction of good unless forced by necessity', and 'since men are bad and will not observe it [faith] with you, you also need not observe it with them', from *The Prince* (1513). His claims that politicians should be governed by expediency not morality, and that ends justified the means (however inhuman), formed the basis of a new kind of stage villain – ruthlessly egocentric and a master of 'policy', who could both shock audiences and reflect the general disillusionment in Jacobean political life. There was both fear of and fascination for such an inversion of the Christian ideal, as seen in Flamineo's admiration of the Duke of Florence's cunning plots:

> Those are found weighty strokes which come from th'hand,
> But those are killing strokes which come from th'head.
> O the rare tricks of a Machivillian.   (V.3.191–3)

The literary background

Webster's two outstanding tragedies, *The White Devil* and *The Duchess of Malfi*, were performed towards the end of the greatest period of English drama, which had begun some twenty-five years previously with the early plays of Christopher Marlowe (1564–93), Thomas Kyd (1558–94), and John Lyly (*c.*1554–1606). Webster was able to benefit from these earlier dramatists who had established conventions based on a blend of native dramatic traditions and ancient classical models, which together gave Elizabethan drama its peculiar richness and flexibility. He also benefited from a marked improvement in the social status of playwrights which had taken place during this period.

It is in the drama that we find the finest expression of the Renaissance in England. The Renaissance originated in Italy in the fourteenth century with the discovery of forgotten Latin and Greek texts, which triggered off an artistic, literary and scientific revival throughout Europe, and was closely linked with the spread of humanism, which involved a realisation of the full potential and dignity of the human spirit. It was not drama but poetry, however – particularly epic poetry – that was accorded the highest status, and plays were considered ephemeral and slight unless they imitated the highly valued classical models. This famous attack on popular drama by Sir Philip Sidney (1554–86) in his *An Apology for Poetry* (1581–3) demonstrates how it breaks what Webster, in his preface, ll. 17–18, calls 'the critical laws':

> you shall have Asia of the one side, and Afric of the other, and so many other under-kingdoms, that the player, when he cometh in, must ever begin with telling where he is, or else the tale will not be conceived. Now ye shall have three ladies walk to gather flowers and then we must believe the stage to be a garden. By and by we hear news of shipwreck in the same place, and then we are to blame if we accept it not for a rock. Upon the back of that comes out a hideous monster with fire and smoke, and then the miserable beholders are bound to take it for a cave. While in the meantime two armies fly in, represented with four swords and bucklers [shields], and then what hard heart will not receive it for a pitched field?*

The 'true dramatic poem', Webster observes ('To The Reader', l.13), might satisfy classical laws such as the unity of place, but not an audience. The professional dramatist used only those elements of classical formulae which could be assimilated into popular drama. But Webster does seek to ally himself in his preface to *The White Devil* with what could be styled 'gentleman' playwrights, often university-trained, steeped in the ancient authors, perhaps with alternative sources of income, who were more conscious of classical precedent. Thus he places

*G. Shepherd (ed.): *An Apology for Poetry*, Manchester University Press, 1973, p. 134.

Chapman (1559-1634), Jonson (1572-1637), Beaumont (1584-1616), and Fletcher (1579-1625) before the professional men of the theatre, Shakespeare (1564-1616), Dekker (*c*.1572-1632) and Heywood (*c*.1573-1641). His plays follow the classical precepts for tragedies listed by Jonson in his preface to *Sejanus* (1603): 'truth of argument, dignity of persons, gravity and height of Elocution, fulnesse and frequencie of Sentence [moral comments]'. Many of the features of popular drama attacked by Sidney, particularly multiplicity (number and variety of events, characters, scenes and times) and sequential action (narrating a story from start to finish rather than beginning in the middle as does Greek drama) are to be found in *The White Devil*. In fact this play ignores the current trend towards more courtly entertainments involving song and dance.

Another element of Renaissance humanism which greatly influenced the nature of English literature at this time was the emphasis placed in education on the study of rhetoric, which can be defined as the body of aims, definitions, prescriptions and rules taken from classical authors to govern man's use of language in both speech and writing. We can see rhetorical formulae at work in the Sidney passage above, for example in the repeated 'and then' clauses, which play a major part in persuading us of the truth of Sidney's argument. Early Elizabethan plays are characterised by their fondness for such repeated verbal patterns, together with figures of speech and other elaborate and decorative structures. There was less use of highly formalised rhetoric by Webster's time, although it does occur in *The White Devil*:

VITTORIA: You did name your duchess.
BRACHIANO: Whose death God pardon.
VITTORIA: Whose death God revenge!

(IV.2.104-5)

Rhetorical set speeches had given way to increasingly sophisticated techniques based on stage action, a more structural use of imagery (see pp. 44-5) and dramatic dialogue, employing speech of a more everyday nature and making rhetorical patterns relate more closely to the speaker's character. Thus we find in *The White Devil* that purely decorative rhetoric, such as that used by the lawyer in the trial scene, is treated with suspicion and scorn.

A note on the text

The text of *The White Devil*, first published in 1612, presents few of the problems which are often found in early dramatic texts. This is because it was almost certainly prepared for and seen through the press by Webster himself. It was unusual for this to happen as plays were still considered by many to be too slight to warrant publication, and certainly not for the purpose of self-advertisement by the author. Webster is slightly defensive about publication, writing in his preface 'To The Reader', ll. 1–2, 'In publishing this tragedy, I do but challenge to myself that liberty, which other men have ta'en before me'. Webster, it appears from this preface, wished his play to be regarded as a serious work of literature and wanted to offset its poor reception on the stage.

Play manuscripts at this time tended to come by way of the theatre companies, who sold them when they passed out of repertoire, or during plague visitations when money was short. Some plays were stolen or taken down in shorthand during a performance. The author had no control over publication because there were no copyright laws, nor could a company prevent the performance of one of its plays by a rival company; hence it was against its interests to publish valued play scripts. There are some strange features about this text which suggest that the text which Webster gave the printer was a private manuscript that had not been altered by the theatre company. For example, it has no act or scene divisions unlike all surviving playhouse scripts of that time; and there are numerous errors in the stage directions, including the names of four characters who have no lines or actions in the play. J. R. Brown, in the edition recommended below, conjectures that Webster made some hasty changes to a manuscript in which the play's dialogue was accurate but the action incomprehensible, because the playhouse had not prepared it for performance. Three more editions of the play were called for in the seventeenth century: in 1631, 1665 and 1672.

As modern editions have different line numbers, it is necessary to refer to one particular edition in these Notes. The following is the best and is easily available in paperback:

JOHN WEBSTER: *The White Devil*, ed. by J. R. Brown in the Revels Plays series, London, 1960; rpt. Manchester University Press, 1979.*

*Note that the name Brachiano may, be spelled either 'Brachiano' or 'Bracciano', according to the different editions of the text. The spelling adopted in these Notes follows the first edition of the play and is intended to represent the Italian pronunciation of the name. The edition recommended here prefers the alternative spelling.

Part 2

Summaries
of THE WHITE DEVIL

A general summary

The powerful Duke of Brachiano is passionately in love with Vittoria Corombona, whose brother, Flamineo, assists the duke's suit. Flamineo arranges the murder of Brachiano's wife, Isabella, and Camillo, Vittoria's foolish husband; thus arousing the wrath of Isabella's brother, Francisco de Medici, and Camillo's uncle, Cardinal Monticelso. They have Vittoria brought to trial for murder and adultery and she is sentenced to confinement in a house for reformed prostitutes in Rome. Brachiano rescues her and they flee to Padua to be married, as a result of which they are excommunicated by Monticelso, who has been elected Pope. Francisco plots their deaths with the aid of a certain Lodovico, who has a grievance against Flamineo and was in love with Isabella. They attend Brachiano's wedding celebrations in disguise and have him poisoned and then strangled in his bed. After the triumph of the marriage Flamineo's fortunes are also waning. He murders his own brother, Marcello, an act which drives his mother, Cornelia, into madness. His mistress, Zanche, betrays him to the disguised Francisco and Vittoria refuses to reward him for his services. Flamineo pretends suicide to test his sister's feelings and exposes her hatred for him as she triumphs over his body. At this point Lodovico enters with other conspirators and they murder Flamineo, Vittoria, and Zanche. Before they can escape, however, they are caught and sent for punishment by Brachiano's young son and successor, Giovanni.

Detailed summaries

To the Reader

Webster's purpose in attaching a preface to his play for publication is fourfold. Firstly, he wishes to explain the failure of the play when it was first performed at the Red Bull playhouse, a poor theatre with an ignorant audience. Secondly, he admits that he has failed to follow classical rules of composition but blames this also on the low taste of the audience. Thirdly, he defends himself against the charge of slow writing as such care is the basis of excellence; and fourthly, he pays homage to those contemporary playwrights whom he most admires.

NOTES AND GLOSSARY:

challenge:	claim
nos . . . nihil:	(*Latin*) 'we know these things are nothing', from an epigram by the poet Martial, who was born in Spain *c*.AD40 and died *c*.AD104
Nec . . . Molestas:	'you [the poet's book] will not fear the mocks of the malicious, nor provide wrapping for mackerel.' By Martial; see previous note
non . . . dixi:	'you cannot say more against my trifles than I have said myself.' By Martial; see previous note
Nuntius:	(*Latin*) messenger
O . . . ilia:	(*Latin*) 'O strong stomachs of harvesters'. From a poem by Horace, a celebrated Roman poet, 65–8BC; see 1.23
Haec . . . relinques:	'What you leave today will be for the pigs to eat.' By Horace; see previous note
Euripides:	A famous Greek dramatist, author of about ninety-two plays, *c*.480–406BC
Chapman . . . Heywood:	a list of some of the most successful of Webster's contemporary playwrights: George Chapman (*c*.1560–1634), Ben Jonson (1572–1637), Francis Beaumont (1584–1616), John Fletcher (1579–1625), William Shakespeare (1564–1616), Thomas Dekker (*c*.1572–1632), and Thomas Heywood (*c*.1573–1641)
non . . . mori:	(*Latin*) 'these monuments do not know how to die'. By Martial; see note to 1.3

Act I Scene 1

Count Lodovico has been banished from Rome. Although he admits to having committed various crimes, he feels that he has been victimised by powerful enemies. His friends Gasparo and Antonelli seem to make fun of his discomfiture and tell him to bear his misfortune with patience. Lodovico, however, threatens violent revenge. In passing we are told that the Duke of Brachiano is trying to seduce Vittoria (though her response is left unclear and remains so), and Lodovico's bitter rage turns partly against her, as her influence with the duke could have secured his pardon.

NOTES AND GLOSSARY:

Democritus:	a Greek philosopher (460–370BC) known as the 'laughing philosopher', traditionally placed next to Heraclitus (*c*.540–*c*.475BC), the 'weeping philosopher'
quite:	reward

wolf ... hungry:	only the hungry poor appear wolf-like; the wolfish nature of the rich is disguised. This is the first of many images relating humans and beasts
mummia:	wax used in embalming and deemed to have medicinal value
kennel:	gutter
caviare:	the eggs of the sturgeon fish, a rare delicacy
phoenix:	the rarest of foods, as it was believed that only one such bird was alive at any one time and that its descendant rose from the ashes of the dead predecessor
meteor ... earth:	a corrupt element drawn from the earth by the sun and becoming vapour; meteors were regarded as symbolic of change and decay
This ... buckets:	that is, the full content of the speech is shared between Gasparo and Antonelli
have a full man within you:	be totally self-sufficient
painted:	apparent, not real: a central theme in the play
cut-works:	open-work embroidery
make use of it:	profit by the experience
(*sennet*):	a sounding of trumpets

Act I Scene 2

Brachiano declares that he is passionately in love with Vittoria. His secretary, Flamineo, who is Vittoria's brother, promises to aid him and advises him how he can best obtain his pleasure. It is Flamineo, with his cynical commentary, who dominates and sets the tone of the scene. Brachiano withdraws when Camillo, Vittoria's jealous but foolish husband, appears. Camillo also makes Flamineo his confidant, complaining of his wife's coldness, and Flamineo undertakes to reconcile them. When Vittoria enters, he pretends to persuade her to go to bed with her husband, while actually procuring her for his master, Brachiano. He tricks Camillo into locking himself into his room for the night to clear a path for Brachiano, who emerges from his hiding-place and professes his love for Vittoria. Under the pretext of recounting a 'foolish idle dream' she suggests to the duke that he murder his own wife and Camillo. He accepts the suggestion, but at this point Cornelia, the mother of Vittoria and Flamineo, who has been eavesdropping, enters and upbraids her children and the duke. Her curses drive off Vittoria and the disappointed duke, but Flamineo justifies his actions and accuses his mother of not providing for him and so forcing him to seek preferment by any means. Cornelia's interruption is crucial as it marks a turning point in the action: we now wait for the curse to take effect.

NOTES AND GLOSSARY:

caroche:	a large coach
buttery:	store-room for drinks and general provisions
gilder . . . quicksilver:	the process of gilding caused poisonous vapour to rise from mercury, which caused insanity
liver:	the supposed seat of the passions
barriers:	used to separate combatants fighting to entertain the court
feathers:	plumes struck from the combatants' helmets
shed hairs:	perhaps as a result of treatment for venereal disease
Irish . . . venturous:	that is, Camillo would be as ready to stake his virility (having none)
Dutch . . . breeches:	Dutch fashion was tight shirts and baggy trousers; the shrinking has a sexual implication
under-age protestation:	immature wooing
foot-cloth:	a cloth which covered horses' backs and was considered a sign of dignity; the use of 'asides', as in this speech, gives Flamineo a special relationship with the audience
count:	a bawdy pun
bowler . . . jump:	Camillo's quibbles refer to the game of bowls. In bowling 'booty' two players combine against a third (booty also = plunder). The 'cheek' is the round surface of the bowl; the 'bias' is a weight in its side; the 'mistress' is the jack at which the bowls are aimed; to 'jump with' is to run up against, also to lie with
Aristotle:	a Greek philosopher (384–322BC) pupil of Plato (c.429–347BC) and tutor of Alexander the Great (356–323BC)
ephemerides:	almanac or calendar containing predictions
boy you:	be with you
horn-shavings:	horns were said to grow on cuckolds' foreheads
God refuse me:	(an oath) May God cast me off
but:	except
leon:	leash
wrings:	pinches (due to tightness round his cuckold's horns)
Jacob's staff:	an instrument for measuring heights
mutton:	(slang) loose women
provocative electuaries:	aphrodisiacs
uttered:	put up for sale
Jubilee:	the year of Jubilee instituted in 1300; it was a time for obtaining indulgences for acts of piety; the most recent Jubilee year would have been 1600

Ida:	a sacred range of mountains near Troy
Corinth:	a Greek trading centre famous for its expensive wares and its prostitutes
carved ... capon:	castrated cock, therefore a eunuch
black-guard:	the lowest servants
tickle:	arouse, provoke; Camillo's ignorance of what the audience knows to be going on here is a good example of what is called 'discrepant awareness', some observers knowing more than others; it is a common dramatic technique
sage:	a quibble on (i) a herb used in cooking, and (ii) wisdom; calves = young fools
crouching ... hams:	squatting in a position of humility
glass-house:	a factory making glass
foil:	setting for a jewel
philosopher's stone:	alchemists sought this mythical stone, which was supposed to turn base metal to gold, prolong life, and cure diseases
breese:	gadflies, which sting
tumultuary:	irregular, hastily formed
quae negata grata:	(*Latin*) 'what is denied is desired'
adamant:	a magnet
progress:	a journey undertaken by a monarch
jewel:	a pun on virginity or precious parts
yew:	a pun = 'you'; the yew tree was associated with death
cross-sticks:	possibly wooden crosses stuck in a grave, or reeds crossed to protect or bind a grave together
phlegmatic:	Elizabethans believed the body to be governed by a blend of four humours, each associated with the four elements – earth, air, fire or water – and one's character to be determined by the dominance of one humour. Here Brachiano's duchess is said to be of the watery humour (other humours are melancholic, choleric and sanguine), and hence cold
Fury:	in classical mythology the Furies are the three avenging goddesses, Tisiphone, Megaera and Alecto, who were sent from hell to avenge wrongs
Thessaly:	a district of Northern Greece renowned for poisonous herbs; the garden was commonly used as a metaphor for a country, offering parallel effects of good and bad management
dials:	sundials
beard ... stirrup:	be a mounted attendant and not a mere footman

Padua:	an Italian city famous for its university
conspiring . . . graduate:	means either that he graduated by losing his youth, or by corrupt conspiracy with an older member of the university
Lycurgus:	an Athenian orator and statesman, *c.*396–*c.*324BC

Act II Scene 1

Francisco, Duke of Florence (Brachiano's brother-in-law) and Cardinal Monticelso (Camillo's kinsman) have resolved to effect a reconciliation between Brachiano and his wife, Isabella, who has just arrived in Rome. With Isabella absent from the room they lecture Brachiano on his moral responsibilities and eventually charge him with adultery with Vittoria. He flies into a rage but is pacified with the entrance of his son, Giovanni, and he is left alone with his wife. Despite Isabella's professions of love, Brachiano harshly rejects her and accuses her of inciting Francisco and the Cardinal against him. He vows a perpetual divorce from her, but, in order to protect him, Isabella claims responsibility for the rift. Brachiano, presented unsympathetically throughout this scene, now orders a hired poisoner to murder his wife, and Flamineo promises to have Camillo killed. Francisco and Monticelso arrange for Camillo to be absent from his home so as to draw Brachiano more deeply into his adulterous affair with Vittoria, for they hope that this will lead to his ruin.

NOTES AND GLOSSARY:

dove-house:	ironic, as doves were proverbially guileless and tame
pole-cats:	strong-smelling predatory animals, fond of pigeons and poultry
previous . . . straying:	a circle of powdered unicorn's horn was thought to be able to stop a spider moving from within, as Isabella wished to hold Brachiano; such horns were very expensive
sting . . . tail:	adders were supposed to be able to sting with both mouth and tail
fetch a course about:	turn from pursuit of the prey
shift:	change
cloth of tissue:	rich cloth woven with gold or silver thread
hemlock:	a poisonous plant
Switzers:	Swiss mercenaries, often hired by Italian rulers
ghostly father:	spiritual priest (anticipating Brachiano's death-bed torments in Act V Scene 3)
crackers:	fireworks, used for entertainment

change . . . plasters: that is, exchange indulgence for disease

triumph: in ancient Rome a solemn procession in honour of a victorious general, including such spectacles as wild-beast fights

Tiber: the river on which Rome stands

wild-ducks: prostitutes

moulting-time: the end of the mating season; also a reference to venereal disease causing baldness

tale of a tub: a far-fetched tale; also a reference to the sweating-tub used in curing veneral disease

express . . . reason: obscure: it may mean 'give a commonsense explanation to my verse'

Homer's . . . bulrush: from *The Battle of Frogs and Mice* attributed to Homer (the poet, supposedly blind, regarded by the Greeks as the author of the *Iliad* and *Odyssey*, dated some time before 700BC); the frogs use bulrushes as spears in the battle

Dansk: Danish; famous for playing drums

lapwing: the type of precocity

Italian: Italians were proverbially jealous

breath . . . physic: Isabella's scented breath is associated by Brachiano with the methods used to keep the air free from plague infection

great duke: a sneer at Francisco's title of Grand Duke of Tuscany

I scorn . . . Polack: 'I scorn him as worthless'. Poles were reported to shave their heads close and to attach slight importance to human life

winding sheet: the cloth wrapped around a corpse

Fury: there were three Furies in classical legend, Tisiphone, Megaera and Allecto, who punished sin, especially the murder of kin

mummia: compare note to I.1.16

manet . . . repostum: (*Latin*) 'It shall be treasured deep within my mind', from the *Aeneid* by Virgil, a famous Latin poet, 70–19BC

horns upon thee: that is, I hope your husband is unfaithful (reference to cuckold's horns)

turn in post: return quickly

bring down her stomach: reduce the swelling caused by hysterical passion

stibium . . . cantharides: types of poison

to Candy: to his death; Candy = Crete, where men were reputed to feed on poisonous snakes

quack-salving: acting like a spurious doctor

should ... execution:	when sentenced to whipping for lechery he pretended that he had already been sentenced for debt, but though he escaped the whipping, another rogue, pretending to be the creditor, made him pay according to the supposed judgement against him
ventages:	holes
cornet:	a musical instrument with numerous holes
lamprey:	an eel-like fish reputedly having nine eyes
Ireland:	reputed to have no poison because St Patrick collected all the venomous beasts and cast them into the sea
vapour ... Dublin:	an allusion to a Spaniard, Don Diego, who made himself obnoxious in St Paul's Cathedral in London
St Anthony's fire:	a disease called erysipelas which causes red skin on the face; possibly also slang for breaking wind
chirurgeon:	surgeon
engine:	means, contrivance
gallowses ... shoulders:	those fit for hanging in Holland, placed on a man's shoulders who then moves away
Inopem me copia fecit:	(*Latin*) 'Abundance has made me destitute', from the *Metamorphoses* by the famous poet Ovid, 43BC–c.AD17
Jupiter:	in Roman mythology the god of the sky and king of the gods
ranger:	game-keeper, with a second meaning of rake or libertine

---

Act II Scene 2

Brachiano employes a magician, who in two dumb shows lets him see how the murders of Isabella and Camillo are performed; the former by means of a poisoned portrait of her husband which Isabella lovingly kisses, and the latter during exercise on a vaulting horse when Flamineo breaks his neck.

NOTES AND GLOSSARY:

nigromancer:	devil-inspired magician; associating with such a person would link Brachiano with damnation in the mind of a contemporary audience
windmills:	unrealistic schemes
curtal:	a reference to a horse called Morocco which was exhibited in London in the 1590s and could perform tricks; his master was believed to possess magical powers
figure-flingers:	casters of horoscopes

fustian:	pretentious
(**dumb show**):	a medieval device used by Webster and his contemporary playwrights to telescope time and allow a juxtaposition of action and commentary; here we can witness and contrast both the grotesque deaths and Brachiano's revoltingly heartless response

Act III Scene 1

Vittoria is to be put on trial for her infamous way of living. Flamineo and his brother Marcello have a discussion and Marcello urges his brother to become honest, but Flamineo mockingly observes that his brother's honesty has brought scant rewards. The ambassadors who have been invited to the trial arrive, and Flamineo comments satirically on their appearance. This scene enables us to observe together and evaluate almost all the characters in the play.

NOTES AND GLOSSARY:

lieger:	resident
in ... week:	caught in a trap
catch conies:	cheat fools; also referring back to 'ferret' in the previous line, an animal which hunts rabbits (conies)
chamois:	the jerkins of this soft leather which soldiers wore beneath their armour
builder:	employed for building
mandrake:	a poisonous plant with a forked root resembling the human form; supposed to grow under gallows and to feed off blood, shrieking if pulled from the ground
proffers:	pretends to hit
poulter:	poulterer; poulterers went to market so early that they often fell asleep on horseback (also, in this context = whore's back – tilting having a sexual innuendo)
face in's ruff:	a reference to the enormous ruffs which Spaniards favoured, worn around the neck
cypress:	cobweb material often worn as a hatband

Act III Scene 2

Brachiano attends the trial of Vittoria without invitation. She defends herself ably and makes the prosecuting lawyer look ridiculous. He is dismissed and Monticelso, despite being judge, takes over the prosecution. The murder of Camillo is referred to, but there is insufficient evidence for a charge to be brought, so Monticelso concentrates on proving her morally corrupt. Brachiano, after admitting he had spent the night of Camillo's death in Vittoria's house, storms out of the courtroom in a rage. Vittoria skilfully pleads her innocence but is found guilty of immoral conduct and sentenced to imprisonment in a house of penitent whores. Immediately after the trial Francisco and Monticelso learn that Isabella has also been murdered. Webster reminds us, in the contrast between Brachiano's hypocritical and Giovanni's genuine grief, of crimes (in which Vittoria is implicated) which are never brought to trial.

NOTES AND GLOSSARY:

Domine ... corruptissimam: (*Latin*) 'My lord, observe this plague, the most corrupted of women'

give aim: tell him how close to the mark (target) his shots (accusations) are

literated ... projections: the lawyer's language is so strained and artificial that little sense can be made of it

to Latin: compared with Latin

fustian: (i) coarse cloth (ii) inflated language; the bag is in fact made of buckram, a kind of stiff, coarse linen

effected: put into effect; perhaps this is a misprint for 'affected' = desired

Sodom and Gomorrah: the two cities destroyed by God because of the vices of the inhabitants; there is an ancient idea that fruits which grew in these places appeared fair but were bitter; see the Bible, Deuteronomy 32:32

envenom'd Pothecary: that is, the lawyer

scarlet the colour both of the cardinal's robes and the lawyer's

character: this type of analysis, based on the classical models of Theophrastus (*c*.372–*c*.287BC), was very popular in seventeenth-century literature, and Webster almost certainly contributed to a collection called *New Characters* by Sir Thomas Overbury (1581–1613), the relevant edition of which was published in 1615

coz'ning alchemy: from the Middle Ages onwards cheats had preyed on greedy victims who wished to turn base metals into gold, although some respected scientists were also alchemists

Low Countries ... exactions: at this time taxes on some things in the Netherlands exceeded the original value of the commodity

bodies ... surgeons:	corpses acquired by surgeons for instructing students in human anatomy
Tartar:	barbarian; but more specifically meaning the Mongolian horde which overran Asia and part of Europe in the Middle Ages
Perseus:	in classical mythology, the son of Zeus and Danae who cut off the head of Medusa, a snake-headed monster
strict-combined:	closely (possibly secretly) allied
of thy coat:	of your profession
challenge:	claim
valance:	bed-curtain
demi-foot-cloth:	a cloth which half covered a horse
moil:	mule
Nemo ... lacessit:	(Latin) 'No-one harms me with impunity'
Casta ... rogavit:	(Latin) 'She is chaste whom no-one has tempted'
crusadoes:	Portuguese coins of gold or silver
choke-pear:	rough and unpalatable pear
Vitelli:	a well-known Roman family
julio:	coin of Pope Julius II (1503–13) of small value
ballated:	balladed
play's a'th'stage:	topical scandals were often presented on stage; in 1624 Webster himself collaborated in such a play, entitled *The Late Murder of the Son upon the Mother* which concerned a friend of Webster's father
convertites:	reformed prostitutes
lost too much:	that is, by the death of his sister, Isabella
gave me suck:	fed me at her breast; an uncommon practice among the aristocracy as mothers feared ensuing damage to their figures

Act III Scene 3

Flamineo, having decided to pretend to be mad to avoid suspicion, meets Lodovico, who has returned to Rome from exile to seek a pardon. They both conceal their feeling behind a mask of fashionable melancholy to find out each other's intentions, but they fall out violently when Lodovico hears of his pardon; Flamineo strikes him for insulting Vittoria, and they have to be separated to avoid a brawl.

NOTES AND GLOSSARY:

pedlars in Poland:	in the seventeenth century Poles were apparently very poor, and there were many pedlars (street vendors) in the country
piles:	(i) wooden supports (ii) haemorrhoids

politician:	crafty and scheming intriguer
backside:	supposedly kissed by witches in token of their obedience to the devil
diversivolent:	setting others at variance (copied from the lawyer in the previous scene, III.2.28)
gudgeons:	small fish, simpletons
weights . . . with:	a form of torture applied to those who refused to plead guilty or not guilty
well may:	with good reason
six benefices:	pluralism (the holding of more than one church living) was common in England at this time
Wolner:	a famous Elizabethan glutton
stigmatic:	deformed, ill-favoured
wish . . . dog-days:	that is, I wish thee an eternal season of heat and lust (dog-days) best suited for pandering
faggots:	bundles of sticks
taffeta:	supposedly louse-proof underclothes
grieve:	ironic; they enter laughing
girn:	(i) rogue (ii) snarl, grimace
strappado'd:	hung up by the hands, which have been tied across the back
felly:	part of a wheel's rim
break:	break your oath

Act IV Scene 1

Monticelso tries to persuade Francisco to revenge his sister's death, but Francisco does not trust the Cardinal and disclaims any such intention. However, he borrows from Monticelso a 'black book' containing the names of all the criminals in Rome, in order to find suitable tools for his vengeance. Calling up a vision of his dead sister, Isabella, he meditates upon revenge, and decides to write a letter to Vittoria professing love, to create mischief between her and Brachiano. He also decides to employ Lodovico as a murderer.

NOTES AND GLOSSARY:

fowler:	one who hunts birds
intelligence:	secret information
jealous:	suspicious, watchful
taking up commodities:	to lend articles in place of money, putting an artificial value on them, then require cash repayment at the inflated evaluation
politic bankrupts:	clever swindlers who claim bankruptcy after heavy borrowing and avoid repayment

fellows ... children: men who arrange lovers for their wives and force them to buy goods at inflated prices in return for silence about their immorality

share ... reportage: give a reward to scriveners for recommending them to the usurer's customers

antedate ... writs: fake the evidence in order, perhaps, to enforce a writ of execution more quickly

tribute of wolves: King Edgar (AD944–975) is supposed to have exacted from the Welsh a tribute of three hundred wolves a year to rid the land of wild animals

laundress: laundresses were notoriously lascivious

idleness: foolishness

halts: limps

Irish ... head: reputedly the Irish of Webster's day would not believe an enemy dead until they had cut off his head

Flectere ... movebo: (*Latin*) 'If I cannot prevail upon the gods above, I will move those of the infernal regions', from Virgil's epic poem the *Aeneid*; like Brachiano, Francisco allies himself with the forces of darkness

Act IV Scene 2

As Francisco had intended, his spurious love-letter to Vittoria is intercepted by Brachiano, who, in a jealous fury, quarrels with Flamineo and insults Vittoria. She reminds him that her present dilemma is very different from what he had promised her, denies any involvement with Francisco and throws ·herself upon a bed, in tears. Brachiano is contrite and, with Flamineo acting again as pander and adviser, he is reconciled with Vittoria. It is resolved to smuggle her out of the house of convertites in disguise. Flamineo, however, is growing restless as he feels that his services to Brachiano are producing no tangible reward.

NOTES AND GLOSSARY:

cut it up: that is, cut through the crust on a pie

lees: sediment deposited at the bottom of wine

equivocation: use of words with double meanings, such as 'hang' and 'halter' = nose

bed-straw: used in place of mattresses; straw helped in ripening fruit

lines of age: wrinkles

line convinces: this love poem confutes

atomies: pieces as small as motes of dust

O'er ... water: in a difficult position; Flamineo puns (compare 'wearing' 1.49) on 'changeable' = 'shot' as in 'watered or shot silk'

run: quibble on the 'running' of a sore

neck broke: a threat to repeat the method used to murder Camillo

Russia: this refers to the practice in Russia of punishing debtors by beating on the shins

look ... sallet: expect to be poisoned; the English associated Spain and Italy with poison as a favoured method of killing; this one of many references in the play to poisoning

Polyphemus to Ulysses: Ulysses is the hero of the *Odyssey* by the Greek poet Homer, written before 700BC, and Polyphemus is one of a race of one-eyed giants called Cyclops, who plans to kill Ulysses and his followers after having offered hospitality

turves: pieces of turf

characters nor hieroglyphics: that is, the meaning of the letter is clear and does not need decoding

receiver: pimp

reclaimed ... bells: terms from hawking: to 'reclaim' was to call back a hawk (with a pun on saving from an evil course), and bells were tied to a hawk's legs to aid recovery and to frighten prey

hawk: in this context meaning swindler (that is, Francisco)

devil in crystal: a probable allusion to the play's title; the phrase suggests deception; it was widely believed that devils could be trapped in crystal

adamants: magnets

Irish funerals: a reference to the practice of keening, a type of wailing lamentation to be heard at funerals in Ireland

palsy ... foxes: foxes were used as a cure for paralysis

not matches: squinted and hence unattractive

forwardness: perversity

leverets: young hares

quat: squat, still

broom-men: street-sweepers

use: usury, interest

ferret ... blowing: a superstition that ferrets will loose their grip if blown upon

shoot: sail across

still: always, continually

Grecians ... wooden horse: a reference to the device used by the Greek army to gain access to Troy by hiding in a huge hollow horse made of wood. This brought to an end the ten-year Trojan War which is the subject of Homer's famous *Iliad* written before 700BC

Barbary: used by Elizabethans to describe the whole of Africa's north coast west of Egypt; it was associated with barbaric savagery

amain: at once, with all speed

Nilus: the river Nile in Egypt; the following fable is not Webster's invention

---

Act IV Scene 3

The old Pope has died and a papal election is held, resulting in the selection of Cardinal Monticelso as Pope. As he is speaking his benediction to the crowd Francisco informs him of Vittoria and Brachiano's flight to Padua, and the Pope immediately excommunicates them. After the ceremonies the new Pope becomes suspicious on seeing Francisco and the notorious Lodovico in conversation. He manages to draw from Lodovico the fact that he plans to revenge Isabella's murder as he had had a passion for her. Monticelso condemns this intent, but Francisco sends for Lodovico in the Pope's name and so tricks him into believing the Pope supports his planned revenge, and this fires his enthusiasm for the deed.

NOTES AND GLOSSARY:

Rhodes: The order of the Knights of St John of Jerusalem, founded during the First Crusade (1096–9), moved to Rhodes, a Greek island

S. Michael: an order founded by Louis XI of France in 1469

Golden Fleece: an order founded by Philip the Good, Duke of Burgundy, in 1430

Holy Ghost: an order founded by Henry III, of France in 1578

Annunciation: the highest order of knights in Italy, founded by Amadeus VI of Savoy in 1362

Garter: the exact date of the foundation of this English order is uncertain, but assumed to be between 1346 and 1348

scrutiny ... admiration: alternative ways of electing a Pope: the former was by voting, the latter (correctly termed 'adoration') was when two-thirds of the cardinals present turned towards and made reverence to a preferred candidate

Denuntio . . . Quartus: (*Latin*) 'I bring you tidings of great joy. The Most Reverend Cardinal Lorenzo di Monticelso has been elected to the Apostolic See, and has chosen the title of Paul IV. (*All*) Long live the Holy Father, Paul IV.' To be historically accurate the title should have been Sixtus V, a hated name to Englishmen as he persecuted Protestants. From this point on, Monticelso is contrasted with the demonic Francisco

Concedimus . . . peccatorum: (*Latin*) 'We grant you the Apostolic blessing and remission of sins'

seat: the technical term for the throne or office of a Pope

career . . . ring-galliard: exercises in the 'manage' of a horse

yew-tree: this reminds us of Vittoria's dream (I.2.233)

Furies: in classical mythology, three avenging goddeses from Hell, called Tisiphone, Megaera and Alecto

---

Act V Scene 1

Brachiano is celebrating his wedding with Vittoria. Among the wedding guests are Francisco, disguised as 'Mulinassar the Moor', and Lodovico and Gasparo, disguised as Capuchin monks ('Franciscans'). A tournament is to take place to mark the occasion and the conspirators plot to murder Brachiano by poisoning his helmet. Flamineo first falls out with Zanche, Vittoria's serving-woman, whom he has tired of as a lover, then defends her against his brother Marcello, who insults and strikes her. Marcello challenges Flamineo to a duel while Zanche begins to cast her eyes on Mulinassar, her supposed countryman.

NOTES AND GLOSSARY:

Duke of Florence: it is a heavy irony that the disguised duke offers his services in a proposed war against himself

barriers: waist-high structures to prevent dangerous close fighting during duels performed for entertainment

seal'd with the sacrament: it is typical of the play that religion and murder should be mixed in this way, a feature which culminates in the death of Brachiano tortured by disguised monks who pretend to give last rites

pommel . . . saddle: Edward Squire was hanged in 1598 for such an act, directed against Queen Elizabeth herself. It is a convention of revenge plays that the manner of taking vengeance should fit the crime

hazards: openings in the inner walls of tennis courts: revengers often wished to destroy soul *and* body. Compare Shakespeare's *Hamlet*, III.3.88–95

casque: helmet

cunning:	magic
Colossuses:	huge statues; derived from the Colossus at Rhodes, a bronze statue of the sun-god, Helios; one of the seven wonders of the ancient world
hung with arras:	with tapestries behind which a man could hide
under his hand:	a signed statement
dog-days:	evil or unhealthy times, associated with hot weather when Sirius, the dog-star, is high in the sky; a time traditionally associated with lust
the disease:	venereal disease; one of many references in this play which is so obsessed with corruption of the flesh as the fruits of lust
Aesop:	a Greek writer of the sixth century BC famed for his animal fables; here Flamineo prefers the body to fine clothes
Westphalia:	now a part of West Germany; the bacon referred to would draw a man to drink as a shoemaker draws on shoes
sunburnt gentleman:	the dark-skinned Mulinassar
haggard:	wild female hawk; a term of abuse meaning 'wanton'
bed-staff:	(i) a staff used for beating the bed when making it (ii) a man in the bed
walnut tree:	proverbially bears more fruit when kicked or beaten
choleric:	the characteristics of one of the four humours; the others are melancholic, sanguine and phlegmatic: they are governed by the dominant presence in the body of yellow bile, black bile, blood, or phlegm, respectively
two . . . ways:	in classical mythology, Eteocles and Polinices fought and killed each other; so great was their enmity that when their bodies were burned together, the flames parted
geese . . . progress:	probably a reference to the prostitutes who attached themselves to royal tours of the country
fit the length on't:	equip himself with one of equal length
Michaelmas:	29 September; late in the year and late in Mulinassar's life

Act V Scene 2

Cornelia, mother of Vittoria and Flamineo, has heard rumours that her other son, Marcello, is about to fight a duel. While Marcello tries to dispel her fears Flamineo enters and runs him through with his own

sword. Cornelia vainly tries to revive him; then tries to protect Flamineo
from the duke's wrath. Brachiano, however, has an old grudge against
Flamineo who braved him earlier in the play, and condemns him to beg
for his pardon every night or face hanging. At the same time, in the
background, Lodovico is ironically passing a death sentence on
Brachiano himself by sprinkling poison on the duke's helmet.

NOTES AND GLOSSARY:

turn your gall up: that is, you are dying (gall denotes bitterness of
spirit)

black lake: the Styx, in classical mythology, a river in Hell; a
further reference to Brachiano's damnation as well
as death

Act V Scene 3

The tournament begins and Brachiano soon feels the effects of the
poison on his helmet, which is so potent that there is no hope of his
recovery. He falls into occasional fits of madness and the disguised
monks, Lodovico and Gasparo, enter to give the last rites. They clear the
bed-chamber to hear Brachiano's confession and then reveal themselves
and taunt the dying man. When Brachiano momentarily recovers and
calls for Vittoria, they strangle him. After his death the court is in
confusion: Vittoria is in despair, Flamineo suspects a plot by the Duke
of Florence, and Zanche offers to betray Vittoria to gain the love of the
disguised Francisco.

NOTES AND GLOSSARY:

beaver: lower portion of the face-guard of a helmet

screech owls: that is, the doctors; owls proverbially foretold death

kiss . . . poison: another of the play's ironies, as it was by kissing him
(that is, his portrait) that Brachiano's wife, Isabella,
was murdered

rough-bearded comet: comets have a beard-like trail; they were supposed
to presage disasters

verge: the area within twelve miles of a king's court

wolf: an ulcer (which devours like a wolf); the real-life
Brachiano had an ulcer in his thigh to which raw
meat was applied as a cure

(*presented in a bed*): here the traverse is drawn to discover Brachiano
and the others on the inner stage

codpiece: clothing covering the crotch area; an appendage to
the close-fitting breeches worn at the time

whipt: trimmed

cuts capers: dances

arras powder:	a white powder which Vittoria would have sprinkled on her hair for the wedding, but is here associated, significantly, with illicit sex ('sinn'd in the pastry')
Domine ... laevum:	(*Latin*) 'Lord Brachiano, you were customarily guarded in battle by your shield; now you shall oppose this shield against your infernal enemy. – With your spear you once conquered in battle; now you shall wield this sacred spear against the enemy of souls. – Listen Lord Brachiano, if you now also approve of what has been done between us, turn your head to the right. – Be assured, Lord Brachiano: think of the good deeds you have done – lastly remember that my soul is pledged for yours if there should be any danger. – If you now also approve what has been done between us turn your head to the left'
sallets:	poisons
winter plague:	particularly virulent, as plagues generally ended with the hot summer weather
woman-keeper:	nurse; such were often suspected of killing patients sick of the plague
pest-house:	a building erected on the edge of the city to house plague victims
moonish:	changeable
Machivillian:	a Machiavellian; as the writings of the Italian author, Machiavelli (1469–1527), were identified with irreligious and unscrupulous cunning of all kinds
saffron:	taken in excess it was believed to cause death by laughter
sad dream:	compare the implications of Vittoria's dream in Act I Scene 2
bed:	thick entanglement
laurel:	bestowed for famous achievements, but also supposedly used by partridges as a purgative

Act V Scene 4

The young Prince Giovanni, the son of Brachiano and Isabella, forbids Flamineo access to the presence-chamber. Flamineo then goes to see his mother who is busy winding Marcello's corpse, and who has gone mad with the shock of her son's death. Flamineo, ill at ease, next encounters Brachiano's ghost, who indicates that his own death is imminent. Flamineo momentarily feels pangs of remorse, but resolves that

Vittoria, now a wealthy widow, must reward him for his services as her husband promised.

NOTES AND GLOSSARY:

dottrels:	a species of plover; fools, simpletons
Anacharsis:	a Thracian prince of the sixth century BC; confused by Webster with Anaxarchus, a Scythian philosopher, pounded to death in a mortar, and thought erroneously to have laughed at his fate
cullis:	broth
decimo-sexto:	printer's term for a very small book
Castle Angelo:	Castle St Angelo at Rome, where the real Vittoria was imprisoned in 1581–2
smoor:	suffocate
rosemary:	an evergreen herb, hence a symbol of immortality
bays:	a garland of bay leaves was given to poets or conquerors as a token of success; it was supposed to act as a protection against lightning
rue:	a shrub with bitter leaves, associated with regret
heart's-ease:	pansies
(*lily-flowers . . . skull*):	representative of life and death
melancholy:	in Act IV Scene 1 Francisco calls up an image of Isabella 'in a melancholic thought' (1.101), hallucinations being a recognised symptom of melancholy; but Flamineo here claims that the ghost is not a figment of his imagination

Act V Scene 5

In this brief scene, Lodovico persuades Francisco to leave Padua before his disguise is seen through. Francisco accepts this advice, but the conversation is overheard by one of Brachiano's servants, Hortensio, who suspects foul play.

NOTES AND GLOSSARY:

quite:	repay
career:	short gallop at full speed

Act V Scene 6

Flamineo confronts Vittoria and claims his overdue reward for services to Brachiano, but is refused on the grounds that he murdered his brother. Flamineo insists, finally threatening his sister and Zanche with a pair of pistols. Vittoria, aided by Zanche, suggests a suicide pact; ostensibly to escape further revenge from Francisco, but in reality to make away with Flamineo, who agrees to the pact. They duly shoot him, but rather than follow suit they gloat over the apparently dying man (as Lodovico and Gasparo did over Brachiano). Amazingly, Flamineo arises and reveals that the pistols were loaded with blanks. Having exposed their untrustworthiness he prepares to kill them with a second pair of pistols, but he is prevented by the arrival of Lodovico and three other of Francisco's tools. The newcomers tie up Flamineo, his sister and Zanche, stab them, and watch them slowly die. Giovanni and his men break into the chamber, overpower the murderers, and while the still defiant Lodovico is carried off to torture, Giovanni ends the play with a vow that the guilty will be brought to punishment.

NOTES AND GLOSSARY:

ruffin:	devil
blowze:	a ruddy slatternly wench, here applied ironically to the black-faced Zanche
wormwood:	a plant with a bitter taste
Cain:	the first son of Adam and Eve, who committed the first murder, against Abel, his brother, and was cursed by God (see the Bible, Genesis 4:11–15)
patent:	a licence without which a beggar could be arrested and whipped as a vagabond
at a dead lift:	in a tight corner
candied . . . stibium:	all sins except despair are presented with a sugar coating; despair is bitter and poisonous
stop . . . plums:	that is, know when to speak; 'winter plums' must be gathered at exactly the right time
grammatical laments:	laments made according to formal rules
cupping-glasses:	vessels in which a vacuum is created by heating, and then used to draw off blood
Lucian . . . Pippin:	a Greek writer (c.AD115–c.200) whose purgatory, described in his *Menippos*, includes different examples of the ridiculous fates of great men, such as Alexander the great, King of Macedon, 336–323BC; Pompey, a famous Roman soldier and statesman, 106–48BC; Julius Caesar, with Pompey one of the triumvirate who ruled the Roman Empire, eventually becoming a dictator, 101–44BC; Hannibal, a Carthaginian general, famed for taking an army and elephants across the Alps, 247–c.182BC; Augustus, the first Roman emperor, adopted son of Julius Caesar, 63BC–AD14; Charlemagne, Holy Roman Emperor, son of Pepin the Short (here referred to as Pippin – the name of a variety of apple), AD742–814

scruples:	small portions
springe:	snare
fox ... home:	fails to return
braches:	bitches
drive ... body:	suicides were traditionally mutilated thus and then buried at crossroads
Artillery Yard:	a place in London where weekly exercise of arms and military discipline were revived in 1610
Hypermnestra:	in classical mythology one of the fifty daughters of Danaus who swore to kill their husbands in order to protect their father; she alone failed to do so
matachin:	sword-dance
Conceit:	imagination
falling sickness:	epilepsy
fox:	a common name for a sword in Elizabethan England
tent:	probe
blood ... blood:	passion ... life-blood
nine Muses:	in classical mythology the daughters of Zeus and Mnemosyne, who presided over the arts and inspired artistic creation
lions i' th' Tower:	lions were kept in the Tower of London
Candlemas:	2 February
***Haec ... placui*:**	(*Latin*) 'These things will be our reward if I have pleased you'; from an epigram by Martial
Master Perkins:	Richard Perkins, a famous actor in the company of the Queen's Men; he probably played the part of Flamineo

Part 3

Commentary

Date and sources

The White Devil was first published in 1612, and there is evidence of a first performance early in that year. The playwright Thomas Dekker (*c.*1570–1632) wrote in a dedication to the Queen's Men, who had performed a play by him also published in 1612,

> I wish a Faire and Fortunate Day, to your Next New-Play ... because such Brave Triumphes of Poesie, and Elaborate Industry, which my Worthy Friend's Muse hath there set forth, deserve a Theatre full of the very Muses themselves to be Spectators. To that Faire Day I wish a Full, Free and Knowing Auditor.

The 'New-Play' is almost certainly *The White Devil*. Webster was a 'Friend' to Dekker, his work does blend 'Poesie' with 'Industry', and his own preface to *The White Devil* echoes the above passage. As this preface tells us that the play was acted in winter, the most logical placing of the first performance is early in 1612.

The play is based on events in recent Italian history, twenty-seven years having passed since Vittoria Accoramboni's actual death. Her story was of such topical interest that over one hundred separate accounts of it have survived. None of these coincide exactly with Webster's version and it is likely that he used a number of sources, the main one being the same as that found in a newsletter to a German banking house. This has some of the same factual errors as Webster's play – Giovanni for Virginio, the real name of Brachiano's heir, for example – and it ignores Brachiano's obesity, and Vittoria's rumoured suicide attempts, as Webster does.

The fact that there are many discrepancies between Webster's and accurate modern versions of the story is partly due to conflicting sources, but also to the accepted literary convention which authorised the reshaping of history in order to create a formal unity and a higher, more general truth than raw history provided. Where Webster appears to have been deliberately inaccurate one can gain insight into his artistic intentions. For example, he chooses to magnify the involvement of Francisco de Medici, a minor figure in the sources, in order to strengthen the revenge element and to provide a vital link between the two main groups in the play. In the sources Cornelia and Isabella are less than admirable, but Webster gives his play a greater moral clarity by presenting them as virtuous. He gives shape to the formless chronicle of the sources by developing the role of Giovanni who, unhistorically, brings a semblance of order and justice to the end of the play. By altering the sources, moreover, Webster is able to complicate our response to what seem straightforward crimes. Vittoria, for example, is provided with an excuse for adultery by the changing of the virile young husband of the sources into the foolish and impotent Camillo.

There is a peculiar difficulty involved in tracing sources for this author's work, as Webster is one of English literature's greatest borrowers, both in extent and in skilfulness of adaptation. His plays are largely pieced together, in a subtly altered form, from memorable bits of his reading, which he will have jotted down in what was called a 'commonplace book'. The result is that there are innumerable minor sources for a play such as *The White Devil*, one example being his borrowing of the details of the papal election scene from *A Treatise of the Election of Popes* (1605). Though shocking to some modern readers, plagiarism was accepted by Webster's contemporaries, as imitation and embellishment of others' work was conventional and commended.

The Italy of Vittoria Accoramboni

Renaissance England was fascinated by life in Italy, and it was a favourite setting for plays. It was known as the centre of European art, the source of man's greatest creative genius; but paradoxically, it reputedly contained the most underhand and corrupt of courts. Such was the popular image, fuelled by a hatred and suspicion of Roman Catholicism, which provided playwrights with a ready-to-hand image of the workings of evil in a highly-developed civilisation.

Vittoria, born into an old and respected family, was married at sixteen to Francesco Peretti (Webster's Camillo), nephew of Cardinal Montalto (Webster's Monticelso). Some seven years later, childless and unhappy, she met the Duke of Bracciano, who was overweight and twenty years her senior. He was estranged from his wife, Isabella, who by 1576 had taken a lover. During one of Bracciano's rare visits she died (probably strangled by the duke) leaving him free to court Vittoria. In this he was aided by her brother Marcello (Webster's Flamineo), who lured her husband into an ambush in which he was killed. Within a fortnight of Peretti's death in 1581 Vittoria and Bracciano were secretly married, without a religious ceremony. The Pope annulled the marriage, however, and as suspicions about the deaths of Isabella and Peretti increased, ordered Bracciano to send Vittoria home. She was arrested *en route* and confined in a nunnery. Here she attempted to commit suicide when Bracciano appeared to have renounced her, but the duke secretly met her and removed her to his palace for a full wedding ceremony.

Their happiness ended with the election of Montalto as Pope. In 1585 the duke travelled to Rome and tried, without success, to effect a reconciliation with the Pope. Suffering from a malignant ulcer in his leg, he died shortly after his return home. Most of his fortune was left to Vittoria, but the Orsini and Medici families (relatives of Isabella and Bracciano) opposed her inheritance. Lodovico Orsini, a distant cousin and former confidant of Bracciano, forced her to surrender the will, but she cunningly used an earlier document to make the authorities recognise her claim. An infuriated Lodovico returned with an armed gang, dressed fantastically, and broke in upon Vittoria and Flamineo (her younger brother) at prayer. Two men held her and another murdered her brutally while making obscene jests. Flamineo was shot and stabbed to death.

Lodovico and his followers were later seized by the authorities and he was strangled in prison. Marcello was beheaded in 1586 on the order of the Pope. Webster appears to have toned down certain aspects of this bloody tale. According to his main source two of the accomplices in Vittoria's murder 'were riven asunder with red-hot tongs, and killed with a hammer and then quartered'. With its extreme examples of brutality, sexual passion, unscrupulous murder and revenge, this piece of history neatly encapsulated all the commonly held beliefs about life in Italy.

The nature of the play

Revenge tragedy

Webster is a controversial dramatist, viewed at one extreme as second only to Shakespeare, and at the other as a crude sensationalist, responsible for immoral and clumsily structured plays. There is disagreement not only about the artistic integrity of *The White Devil* but also about the nature of the play. This is partly due to Webster's eclecticism, his habit of selecting from numerous sources or models. *The White Devil* appears to make use of several theatrical trends, some of them slightly old-fashioned, to produce a distinctive amalgam which defies categorisation. It has been called, among other things, revenge tragedy, a chronicle play, a family tragedy, a tragedy of love, the tragedy of a whole society, a tragicomedy, and a black farce.

Without doubt, however, *The White Devil* is heavily influenced by the conventions of revenge tragedy. Revenge plays drew on the example of the Roman playwright Seneca (4BC–AD65), who dramatised some spectacularly violent sequences of crime and revenge, and, like Webster, combined bloody and treacherous actions with sententious moralising.

Part of the appeal of Seneca's plays for Elizabethans was their guidance on enduring adversity through fortitude, particularly their presentation of the art of dying well. Such stoicism is a significant feature of Webster's tragedies also. Seneca grew in popularity because he was treating a subject, revenge, which was highly contentious at this time. Private revenge, linked with family honour, was considered by many to be a sacred duty, but this clashed with the Christian ethic which placed revenge in God's hands alone.

Revenge plays were often set in Italy, where, it was believed, the most extreme examples could be found. The writer Thomas Nashe (1567–1601) records that in Italy he 'heard of a box of the ear that hath been revenged thirtie yeares after'. These words contain the basic revenge plot (an offence, a period of delay and then revenge) appealing to playwrights because it solves two great problems: how to begin and how to end a play. *The White Devil* ends in the conventional way: the avengers are disguised, they appear in a 'masque' (a surprise entry of masked revellers), and a figure of authority restores order after the bloody climax. But the revenge element is not so clearly focused in other areas of the play. Lodovico is the main agent of revenge but his motivation seems carelessly presented (for example, II.2.32–4); and the main plotter, Francisco, is a rather shadowy figure who is forgotten by the end of the play. Revenge conventions are being used but are adapted to suit Webster's purpose.

Webster wished to show both revengers and the victims of revenge as evil, the good characters being only on the edge of the action, whereas conventionally the victims were morally inferior. This allowed him to rearrange conventions, for example by making Flamineo, one of the victims, a malcontent who disguises his nature to avoid suspicion, which is a role usually taken by the avenger. Both avengers and victims seek the conventional 'perfect' murder, taking pride in their ingenuity: 'I limb'd this night-piece and it was my best' (V.6.297, and cf. II.2.38) boasts Lodovico. Both factions employ the conventional method, poison, and one from each side sees the conventional ghost (although the ghosts do not trigger off the revenge action as was customary). By making Vittoria, Brachiano and Flamineo more attractive than Francisco and Lodovico, the avengers, Webster reversed the usual flow of sympathy in earlier revenge plays. The genre of revenge tragedy provided Webster with a framework and a number of useful theatrical effects, but he was not attempting to write a revenge play himself, as most of his attention was paid to the relationship between Brachiano, Vittoria and Flamineo, and the latter's satirical commentary, to which the revenge element is far from being central.

Tragicomedy

The sub-title claims that *The White Devil* is the tragedy of Brachiano, but many critics have questioned whether he is the central protagonist, and some have questioned whether the play is a tragedy at all. It can be argued that Vittoria has the strongest claim for centrality as she probably is the 'white devil' of the title; or, this play can be seen as one that has no single hero. In this respect it has been likened to a chronicle, or history play, with which it also shares other characteristics: in the pageantry of the papal election and trial scenes; in its basis in historical fact; and in its sequence of separate events in place of a steady build-up to a single climax. The characters, however, are somewhat too close to being conventional theatrical types rather than realistic historical figures, to allow the play to fit into this category. Critics have sought other descriptions to suit a play without a hero, one of the most appealing of which is the view that it is the tragedy of a society: 'Webster's satirical tragedy looks beyond individuals to the society that shapes them ... The White Devil is not Vittoria Corombona but Renaissance Europe'.*

Webster's play certainly does seem to draw general conclusions about the nature of society and seeks to expose and reform corruption in a harsh way, as we expect of satire, but can the term 'tragedy' be applied to it? Some critics think not, on the grounds that it lacks the general gravity of tone which one associates with that term. It is not that the play lacks deadly serious or highly poignant moments: Cornelia's grief and madness, Brachiano's dying love for Vittoria, and the latter's defiance at her trial and when facing death, are the stuff of which tragedy is made. Webster's technique, however, is to continuously undermine such moments either with satirical commentary (particularly by Flamineo) or with actions which incite laughter and at times border on farce, for example Flamineo's mock-death. In the words of one critic, it is 'a form in which comedy and tragedy, the laughable and the appalling, are so composed that neither is predominant'†; thus it is a tragicomedy.

Such a method is particularly suited to Webster's apparent objective in the play, which is to show that what seems 'white' (that is, pure and virtuous) may be as black as the 'devil'. The dominant tone of the play is one of confused uncertainty, as Webster moves us from one extreme response to its opposite without a breathing space. Such polarisation occurs when we find ourselves laughing at moments of horror: as when Lodovico, ironically disguised as a holy man administering last rites,

*An idea developed by J. Lever; see R. V. Holdsworth (ed.): *'The White Devil' and 'The Duchess of Malfi': a Casebook*, Macmillan, London, 1975, p. 200.
†J. R. Mulryne: 'Webster and the Uses of Tragicomedy' in B. Morris (ed.): *John Webster*, Ernest Benn, London, 1970, p. 135.

wittily taunts the crazed and dying Brachiano; or when Brachiano himself jokes about the horrific poisoning of his wife as he watches her death in a dumb show. Even more striking is the juxtaposition of Flamineo's mock-death with his real death. An audience finds it hard to take the real death with due seriousness when it so closely resembles the comic pretend death. Thus, even death itself, the climax of conventional tragedy, is apparently parodied by Webster. Flamineo's exaggerated death speeches seem to mock the drawn-out deaths of tragic heroes:

> O I smell soot,
> Most stinking soot, the chimney is a-fire, –
> My liver's parboil'd like Scotch holy bread,
> There's a plumber, laying pipes in my guts; – it scalds.
>
> (V.6.141–4)

Throughout the play we come across such comic exaggeration and grotesqueness of both language and action, even at the potentially most solemn moments. Thus Webster uses the standard ghosts of tragedy, but they are received mockingly by those whom they are meant to disturb. This tragicomic technique makes sympathising with personal suffering almost an impossibility, and as we are distanced from individual characters we become more aware of an entire society trapped in a 'mist' of uncertainty (see V.6.260).

The White Devil and morality

Moral lessons are a distinctive feature of this play. Most characters indulge in the proclaiming of such lessons (although only a few minor characters put into practice the spoken moral precepts) in a way which demands special attention. Repeatedly a character's individual manner of expression gives way to a rhyming couplet containing a moral comment of a general nature, an example being Marcello's dying words:

> That tree shall long time keep a steady foot
> Whose branches spread no wider than the root.
>
> (V.2.23–4)

These sentiments are clearly applicable to what has gone before and probably reflect a genuine thought, but often the rhyming *sententiae*, as they are known, seem to be ironically placed and far from genuinely felt, as when Francisco solemnly comments that,

> Treason, like spiders weaving nets for flies,
> By her foul work is found, and in it dies
>
> (IV.1.26–7)

while he *thinks* about how to weave a net to trap Brachiano.

Characters repeatedly strike such noble attitudes which are undermined by the context. As his characters clearly do not act upon the moral precepts they voice, Webster has been accused of disbelieving them himself, and of tagging on to his play a moral doctrine unconnected with the action. It can be argued, however, that Webster's use of *sententiae* makes the audience simultaneously realise the truth of the precepts, which the action as a whole supports, and the irony of their being spoken by villains, whose falsehood they help to expose.

Those who accuse Webster of moral decadence also point to the apparent weakness of those characters in the play who represent virtue in this corrupt society. Cornelia, Marcello, Isabella and Giovanni, it is true, do not make a striking impression, and are not even particularly likeable, as virtue can often seem self-righteous. Webster allows his villains to dominate and even destroy the good characters, until Giovanni's sudden and unconvincing emergence as a power at the end. A typical example is Flamineo's crushing response to Cornelia's surely justified complaint against her son's prostituting her daughter:

> Pray what means have you
> To keep me from the galleys, or the gallows?
> My father prov'd himself a gentleman,
> Sold all's land, and like a fortunate fellow,
> Died ere the money was spent.
>
> (I.2.315–9)

Neither Cornelia nor Marcello are able to compete with Flamineo's articulate cynicism. Nevertheless Webster must have considered the virtuous characters to be a vital element in the play, as he departed drastically from his sources to invent them. Did he include them to mock their virtue or to present an alternative to pervasive corruption? It is difficult to accept that virtue is merely a butt, though whether or not it provides a viable alternative (remembering that Francisco, a main agent of evil, remains unpunished at the end) is a question which the play seems to leave open.

Webster deliberately confuses the moral issues in *The White Devil* by giving morally-unsound characters attractive qualities, and this also has exposed him to the charge of immorality. Moral ambiguity is at the centre of the action: Brachiano and Vittoria are responsible for a horrific double murder but are also filling the romantic roles of the dashing lover and the beautiful, but unfortunately married, mistress. At different points in the play they are presented sympathetically or critically, and this ambivalence continues to the end. We concede it to be just that Brachiano, who poisoned his wife, dies poisoned, while we admire his care for Vittoria; and accept that Vittoria is equally guilty, but are impressed by her fortitude as she faces a cruel death.

Webster's use of imagery

Certain key images recur throughout *The White Devil*; a study of them reveals the dramatist's major concerns. As the title suggests, this is a play about striking contrasts and the deceptive attractiveness of evil. Through the imagery, Webster establishes in the play both the polarisation and the ambiguity contained in the title. We can see this working in the presentation of Vittoria, dazzlingly beautiful yet shockingly corrupt, who attracts such descriptions as 'the devil in crystal', 'If ever the devil did take good shape', 'This whore, forsooth, was holy', 'What goodly fruit she seems.... She'll fall to soot and ashes'.

As with Vittoria's beauty, so Brachiano's greatness is deceptive, and accordingly he attracts imagery which stresses the extreme discrepancy between what a great duke should be and what *this* great duke is:

Some eagles that should gaze upon the sun
Seldom soar high, but take their lustful ease,
Since they from dunghill birds their prey can seize . . .

(II.1.49–51)

The normal meaning of greatness is replaced during the course of the play by a more sinister one:

Both flowers and weeds spring when the sun is warm,
As great men do great good, or else great harm.

(II.2.56–7)

Ultimately to be called 'great' in this play is equivalent to being called 'evil'. As Brachiano says when poisoned: 'There are some great ones that have a hand in this' (V.3.6).

Images of poisoning are at the heart of the play's pervasive contrast between outward appearance and inner reality. Poison cannot be seen and it corrupts inwardly; it is used both metaphorically, as a symbol of man's moral decay, and literally, as an invisible source of death. Hence in the action Isabella kisses lips, which should convey love but, in fact, are smeared with poison. Brachiano similarly puts on a helmet, designed to safeguard him, but ironically 'calls for his destruction' (V.2.80), as the helmet is poisoned. Poisoning seems to be a product of a more general corruption in society, which Webster conceives of as spreading from the court, in a way best described in his play *The Duchess of Malfi*:

. . . a prince's court
Is like a common fountain, whence should flow
Pure silver drops in general: but if't chance
Some curs'd example poison't near the head,
Death, and diseases through the whole land spread. (I.1.11–5)

This sums up the main argument of *The White Devil*: the court appears brilliant, but is both diseased itself and the source of disease in others. Brachiano believes Vittoria to be a 'sweet physician' (I.2.209) but later sees her as the 'curst disease she'll bring me to' (IV.2.46). Vittoria's dream presents Brachiano as a 'sacred yew', which the duke interprets to mean, 'You are lodged within his arms who shall protect you' (I.2.260), but Vittoria later sees this as an illusion: 'I had a limb corrupted to an ulcer,/But I have cut it off' (IV.2.121–2).

The most striking group of related images are those which present this diseased humanity in terms of animal life. The presence of over one hundred animal images suggests that Webster was obsessed with this particular inversion of human potential. Man, placed above animals by God, is fallen, through sin, which 'makes a man a beast' (II.1.138), particularly like the dog and the wolf, which are associated in the play with cowardice, lechery, ferocity, cunning, and fawning. At the start of the play it is said of great men,

> Your wolf no longer seems to be a wolf
> Than when she's hungry. (I.1.8–9)

But woman can also be wolf-like:

> Woman to man
> Is either a god or a wolf. (IV.2.91–2)

To seek preferment at court is likened to mixing with dogs, and 'they that sleep with dogs, shall rise with fleas' (V.1.168). Brachiano's tormentors present a picture of him as a dead dog infested with flies:

> LODOVICO: And thou shalt die like a poor rogue.
> GASPARO: And stink
>   Like a dead fly-blown dog. (V.3.165–6)

It is typical of the jarring effect that the imagery of the play often achieves, that a brilliant nobleman should be presented in this way. The deliberate repetition of such images helps to bind the scenes of the play into a unified whole, continuously forcing home Webster's conception of unseen corruption in the midst of dazzling splendour and apparent nobility.

The structure

The previous section has shown how one of the functions of imagery is to give the play structural coherence, but a charge which is often levelled against *The White Devil* is that it is badly constructed. Webster, it is said, had an eye for the dramatic effectiveness of individual scenes, but was careless about the continuity and overall unity of the action. It is certainly true that the overall impression which the play makes is fragmentary, as a result of the suddenness of the changes of location, of tone, and of character groupings. The arrangement of the plot is dominated by the alternating viewpoint of the two great factions, Brachiano's and Francisco's. The effect of such changing is that the same point of view is never maintained for two successive scenes of the play. The plot has a 'criss-cross' action according to the changing fortunes of the two factions, the opening of Act V marking the peak of fortune for the Brachiano faction, as Flamineo exultingly announces:

> In all the weary minutes of my life,
> Day ne'er broke up till now. This marriage
> Confirms me happy. (V.1.1–3)

The structural criss-crossing allows Webster to make full use of the irony behind claims of security in such a dangerous world, and in this case Flamineo's rise is quickly followed by a fall, which reflects a rise in the fortunes of the revenge group.

Individual scenes themselves undergo abrupt and often ironic changes of direction. Unexpected actions explode into moments of comparative calm, as when Cornelia breaks in upon the courtship of Vittoria by Brachiano:

> CORNELIA [*coming forward*]: Woe to light hearts – they still forerun our
>   fall.
> FLAMINEO: What Fury rais'd thee up? away, away!
> (I.2.269–70)

or in Act V Scene 2 when Flamineo enters, speaks half a line, murders his brother and leaves the stage. The play is characterised by such sudden eruptions so that discontinuity seems to be the norm in the world of the play, a world where not only a character's fortune but his appearance can alter with stunning speed.

Webster appears to have sacrificed a tight structure in order to achieve striking and significant contrasts, both within scenes, as we have seen, and between different scenes. For example, there is an abrupt transition from the magical 'dumb shows', in which the deaths of Isabella and Camillo are presented, to the trial of Vittoria; but if we view the scenes as interrelated, not isolated, Vittoria's impressive self-defence must be set against the two horrific murders which we know she is guilty of inciting. The dramatic structure continually draws our attention to disguise and deceit by placing it next to the real thing, the two often looking equally convincing. In this way Flamineo's mock-death is juxtaposed with his actual death, and Isabella's insincere vow 'never to lie' with Brachiano comes soon after Brachiano's sincere vow 'ne'er more to lie with her', in Act II Scene 1.

One way in which Webster unifies the action is by making dramatic situations echo each other. Early in the play Cornelia prophesies to Vittoria, 'Be thy act Judas-like – betray in kissing' (I.2.298), an idea which is picked up in Act II Scene 2 when Isabella is poisoned by a kiss, and this action is recalled in Brachiano's last coherent remark to Vittoria: 'Do not kiss me, for I shall poison thee' (V.3.26). There is no looseness in construction when the play is looked at from this point of view, but the plot itself does appear rambling. It is based on revenge but has three revengers (one of whom, Monticelso, decides revenge is 'damnable' and drops out, Webster not bothering to explain why) which has a disintegrating effect on the action. There is also an untidy multiplicity of death scenes in the final act instead of a careful build-up to a single climax. Moreover, the action is interrupted by the inclusion of the papal election which has no apparent effect on subsequent events. The indications are that Webster's structural plan was designed to produce suggestive contrasts, often ironic in effect, rather than the chronological succession of events.

The main characters

To some extent characterisation suffers from the same discontinuity as the structure of the plot. The characters tend to be illuminated in flashes which can be plausible and memorable in themselves, but can make a character appear fragmentary or even inconsistent when viewed as a whole. We receive a series of momentary impressions rather than a continuous flow, and at times these impressions are conflicting. Thus, in her four main scenes, Vittoria prompts two murders and commits herself to an adulterous relationship in the first; convincingly and bravely claims innocence and exposes corruption in the second; is emotionally feminine in the third; and full of 'masculine virtue' in the fourth.

Although his characters are carefully individualised (only Camillo and the prosecuting lawyer appear to be stock stage types) Webster wished them to have a representative value. It is for this reason that there is so much generalising commentary in the play, which draws the audience's attention to the universal applicability of the particular action on the stage. This choric commentary, for much of which Flamineo is responsible, makes it difficult for the audience to become emotionally involved with individual characters, as it has an immediately distancing effect. This occurs in Brachiano's potentially moving death-bed scene when the focus moves away from him to include the comments (and witticisms) of those attending on him. Emphasis on the individual and the particular is also lessened by Webster's use in *The White Devil* of pointed parallelisms between characters and character-groupings to bring out similarities or contrasts in behaviour. The three major parallels are Brachiano and Francisco, Flamineo and Lodovico, and Vittoria and Isabella, and these six characters will be considered in turn.

Brachiano

The rulers in Websterian tragedy have perverted the ideal of nobility, which should combine great privilege with great responsibility. Greatness for Brachiano and Francisco means wealth and power, but they neglect social responsibility, with disastrous effects for the well-being of society. That Brachiano is dangerously irresponsible is apparent from his opening words, which must be measured against what is proper for a great man to say and do. For a ruler to be 'quite lost' would be disturbing enough to a Jacobean audience, but to be 'lost' in adulterous love would be shocking. It strikes a chord of moral anarchy and uncertainty which reverberates throughout the play (for example, V.3.35; V.6.174; V.6.248–9; V.6.259–60). This becomes clearer when Brachiano vows to put his lust before maintenance of law, government and family honour:

> I'll seat you above law and above scandal,
> ... nor shall government
> Divide me from you longer than a care
> To keep you great: you shall to me at once
> Be dukedom, health, wife, children, friends and all.
>
> (I.2.263–8)

The impersonal moral 'sentences' which recur in the play condemn rulers who set bad examples. Cornelia reminds Brachiano:

> The lives of princes should like dials move,
> Whose regular example is so strong,
> They make the times by them go right or wrong.
>
> (I.2.287–9; see also II.1.104–7)

Brachiano is weakened by lust. He is at his least impressive in the scenes with Vittoria and Flamineo, who are able to manipulate him. He grows in stature, however, when faced with his great enemies, Francisco and Monticelso, against whom he rages and threatens: 'Defiance! – and I'll meet thee,/Even in a thicket of thy ablest men' (II.1.78–9); 'The sword you frame of such an excellent temper,/I'll sheathe in your own bowels' (III.2.166–7). We find him more attractive also when he shows love for Vittoria on his death-bed:

> Where's this good woman? had I infinite worlds
> They were too little for thee. Must I leave thee?
>
> (V.3.17–18)

Both his bravura and his romance, however, are based on delusions: he is not safe from Francisco even among his own 'ablest men', and Vittoria is hardly a 'good woman'. Webster makes him more sympathetic than in his sources where he is fat and middle-aged with an ulcerous leg, but his amorousness and vigour are only remnants of what might have been: in essence he is a study of sin and its consequences. The play leaves us in no doubt that he is damned, 'given up to the devil', as his murderers say. He sees the devil coming to fetch him as he dies, and has previously linked his damnation to his infatuation with Vittoria:

> How long have I beheld the devil in crystal?
> Thou hast led me, like an heathen sacrifice,
> With music, and with fatal yokes of flowers
> To my eternal ruin. (IV.2.88–91)

The title page presents Brachiano as the tragic hero of the play, but, although he suffers a fall from high status to premature death, he is neither sufficiently heroic nor central enough to the action to fill this role satisfactorily.

Francisco

In a play which is characterised by deception, Francisco stands above all others as the master of disguise and deceit. He is a perfect Machiavellian politician, cold, calculating and ruthless, in contrast with Brachiano who is impetuous and easily led. He plots Brachiano's ruin, first by luring him into 'notorious scandal' (II.1.388) and then, to revenge his sister's death, by arranging his murder. To achieve these ends he employs a range of false poses and disguises. To deceive his brother-in-law he poses as a Christian duke, ironically claiming values which, like Brachiano, he should possess but does not:

> Shall I defy him, and impose a war
> Most burdensome on my poor subjects' necks,
> Which at my will I have not power to end? (IV.1.5–7)

His flexibility and deceptive powers are most apparent when he is disguised as Mulinassar, a Christian Moor. He is able to shift his speech from verse to prose and put on a moralising front which even takes in the perceptive Flamineo. His false rhetoric is so hard to penetrate that Webster had to provide him with two soliloquies to explain his standpoint to the audience, his mistrust of Monticelso (IV.1.37–42) and his plot to trap Brachiano:

> My tragedy must have some idle mirth in't,
> Else it will never pass. I am in love,
> In love with Corombona. (IV.1.119–21)

This also prepares us for his fondness for ironic wit when disguised as Mulinassar (e.g. V.1.106–11). Unlike Brachiano there is an unlikeable coldness about Francisco; he is neither loving nor loved. Of all the many self-centred characters in the play he is the most self-sufficient, the least concerned to form or sustain relationships with others. Perhaps Webster allows him to disappear unpunished from the scene to maintain a consistent portrayal of perfect villainy.

Flamineo

The character of Flamineo is the most impressive of Webster's additions to his source material. While being based on a recognisable stage type, known as a 'tool-villain', he is the most distinctive, as well as being the most consistent, character in the play. Like Francisco he is an egoist, a cynic and a deceiver, but his portrayal is more sympathetic because he is more a victim than an instigator of corruption in society. His father died having wasted his estate, and Flamineo was reared in poverty by his mother:

> For want of means, – the university judge me, –
> I have been fain to heel my tutor's stockings
> At least seven years ...

(I.2.321–3)

Subsequent entry into Brachiano's service corrupted his mind, but he found the only way to 'preferment' open to him was to procure his sister for his master. Bitter, cynical, but worldly-wise, he is an ideal vehicle for Webster to make a satirical commentary on a corrupt society. Much of the action is viewed from his perspective. For example, we never see a liaison between Brachiano and Vittoria that is not observed by Flamineo, and his cynical commentary colours our response and invites us to view it as a crude performance of animal sexuality. He both orchestrates the action and provides an interpretation for the audience. A good example of this is when he makes the following comment on Vittoria's dream:

> Excellent devil.
> She hath taught him in a dream
> To make away his duchess and her husband.

(I.2.256–8)

Objectively we must react to Flamineo's baseness and villainy with disgust and condemnation, but it is difficult to be objective with a character who so often addresses us directly, in asides and soliloquies, and frankly takes us into his confidence. He confesses that he is acting the fool and we delight in his performance:

It may appear to some ridiculous
Thus to talk knave and madman; and sometimes
Come in with a dried sentence, stuff'd with sage.
But this allows my varying of shapes, –
Knaves do grow great by being great men's apes.
(IV.2.243–7; see also III.1.30–1 and III.2.303–8)

He is the main source of humour in the play, often undercutting the
high-flown rhetoric indulged in by other characters. As he takes the
lowest view of humanity, his characteristic speech is a sardonic mockery
of any who have illusions about mankind. Thus when young Giovanni is
praised, Flamineo retorts:

I have known a poor woman's bastard better favour'd
– this is behind him: now, to his face all comparisons
were hateful . . .   (V.4.2–4)

Flamineo lives by his wits in times of great danger, hence he is always on
his guard, tense and living at a pitch of excitement which at times
borders on hysteria.

O let me kill her. – I'll cut my safety
Through your coats of steel: Fate's a spaniel,
We cannot beat it from us . . .

(V.6.176–8)

His agitated speech is always flying off in a new direction, usually
moving, as here, from the particular to the general. His controlled
tension sometimes erupts into violence, as when he kills Marcello or
strikes Lodovico without warning. His experiences have made him
contemptuous of the world; his only moment of admiration is reserved
for his sister, – 'Th'art a noble sister – /I'love thee now' (V.6.241–2), –
for her stoicism in the face of death. This is the moment when she is most
like her brother, Lodovico having numbered him among 'These rogues
that are most weary of their lives' (III.3.130). He is scornful of human
existence and his own exit from life is a predictably light-hearted and
defiant assertion of the one thing in life he trusted in, himself:

I do not look
Who went before, nor who shall follow me;
No, at myself I will begin and end.   (V.6.256–8)

Lodovico

Lodovico has a parallel function to Flamineo in the play. He, too, is
trying to gain a foothold at court by offering his services to a great man,
and he becomes Francisco's tool as Flamineo is Brachiano's. His

character is also similar, being cynical, stoic, crafty, violent and totally unscrupulous. When placed together on stage they appear almost identical, a fact emphasised by Webster when he invents a scene in which they form a short-lived alliance of 'melancholics' (see III.3.59–136). As with Brachiano and Francisco, however, their similarity only breeds enmity.

By providing another satirical commentator in Lodovico, Webster makes Flamineo's jaundiced viewpoint appear more normal (especially when they are joined by numerous other cynical and unscrupulous characters). By making Lodovico more distasteful, he increases our sympathy for Flamineo. The opening scene of the play is dominated by Lodovico and presents him in the worst possible light. He is not a poor man trying to make good, as Flamineo claims in self-justification, but a wealthy man who has 'in three years/Ruin'd the noblest earldom' (I.1.14–15).

Unlike Flamineo he is given no redeeming qualities but begins, as he ends, in unadulterated villainy. He sets the play off on a note of moral chaos from which it never recovers.

Vittoria

If Flamineo is the observer of the play, then Vittoria is the most observed character. She is never on stage alone and is the object of repeated commentary, often of a derogatory nature, by other characters on stage with her. We are continually invited to measure her own words and actions against what is said by observers, and Webster deliberately sets up conflicting impressions as he explores the phenomenon of a 'white devil' or a woman in whom good and evil combine to baffle ordinary moral judgment, as one critic describes her.* Just as she is at the thematic centre of the play, so she is central to the plot as each act can be seen as being devoted to a major phase in her story: Act I – her seduction; Act II – the murders of her husband and of her lover's wife; Act III – her trial; Act IV – her imprisonment and escape; Act V – the deaths of herself and her lover. She has far fewer lines than Flamineo, appears in only five of the sixteen scenes, and says very little until she is placed on trial. If she dominates the play it is because her beauty and attractiveness dominate the minds of the men – not to mention the other women – who seek to blame her for the spread of moral corruption for which they are arguably more responsible.

Our response to Vittoria is complicated from the beginning. Webster departs from historical fact to give her a husband who is a weak and impotent pauper and a lover who is dashing and youthful, so that the pressure on her to be adulterous is great. Nevertheless we are shocked by

*J. R. Brown, (ed.): *The White Devil*, Manchester University Press, 1979, p. xxxvii.

her immodest and cold 'How shall's rid him hence', said of her husband, and the indirect incitement to murder in her account to Brachiano of her 'dream'. With the latter in mind we cannot be unaware of a degree of falsehood and hypocrisy in her trial, although if we were to judge by appearances only she is indeed like a diamond spreading light through darkness, as she claims (III.2.294). However, we *know* that she is not a flawless 'diamond' and, ultimately, her attractiveness for the audience lies principally in her bravery in the face of most powerful enemies:

> I will not weep,
> No I do scorn to call up one poor tear
> To fawn on your injustice . . .
>
> (III.2.284–6)

In her other great scene she is again persecuted by a male, with a similar result, defiance: 'for all thou art worth', she says to Brachiano, 'I'll not shed one tear more' (IV.2.127–8). Despite the magnetism and charm of her personality, however, there is an undercurrent of guilt and corruptness (carried in the imagery with which she is associated, such as 'wolf', 'hawk', 'devil', and 'whore') that undermines her attractiveness and leaves her as a fitting symbol of the paradoxical title of the play.

Isabella

Isabella speaks in merely one scene of the play, her only other appearances being in a dumb show and as an apparition to Francisco. Her significance is more in what she represents than in what she is. Although some critics have found her unattractive, it seems clear that she is presented as a virtuous contrast to Vittoria. In many ways she is her antithesis: a faithful wife and loving mother against Vittoria, the criminal adulteress, a 'withered' 'former beauty' against her present beauty, dull while she is dazzling, virtuous while she is corrupt. Isabella makes sacrifices 'for the weal/Of both your [that is, Brachiano's and Francisco's] dukedoms' (II.1.220–1), whereas Brachiano sacrifices his dukedom for Vittoria. To achieve this polarity Webster departs from his historical sources in which Isabella is far from virtuous.

Her characterisation illustrates Webster's fondness for striking transformations on the stage. Like many of the other characters, albeit for a different purpose, Isabella is able to act out a role which conflicts with her real feelings in order to deceive her listeners:

> To dig the strumpet's eyes out, let her lie
> Some twenty months a-dying, to cut off
> Her nose and lips, pull out her rotten teeth . . .
>
> (II.1.246–8)

She makes such a good job of the rapid change from a devoted to a hatefully jealous wife that one critic at least is 'tempted to think she is indeed that which she seems, '"a foolish, mad,/And jealous woman", perhaps deceiving herself'.*

Other characters

The remaining significant characters – Cornelia, Marcello, Giovanni and Cardinal Monticelso – all end the play apparently opposed to the prevalent corruption, although Monticelso begins on the other side. They all suffer, as does Isabella, from the fact that it is difficult to make simple virtue appealing on the stage; and they all lack the energy, glamour and personal magnetism of the play's sinful characters. Nevertheless they have a vital function in the play, providing an alternative, albeit a fragile one, to the dominant forces of evil.

Monticelso is the least satisfactory character in the play. In the first part he is barely distinguished from Francisco (just as Antonelli and Gasparo merely echo one another), being unscrupulous, worldly (although a churchman), and vengeful. His conduct in Vittoria's trial, where he acts as both judge and prosecuting counsel, is a travesty and reflects badly on him rather than the defendant. But, with no preparation whatsoever, Francisco informs us (in Act IV Scene 1) that Monticelso is not steadfast in revenge; and two scenes later, after his election as Pope, he has changed, it would seem, into a paragon of virtue (see IV.3.80–127).

Neither does Webster appear to have been very concerned with consistency in his portrayal of Giovanni. The young prince begins and proceeds through the play as a rather precocious but entirely innocent child, providing a sentimental interval between murderous plots and arguments. He has a vital structural function to fulfil at the close of the play, however, being needed to establish order and authority after the chaotic lawlessness of the preceding action. Hence after his father's death he appears as a fully-matured and perceptive leader, capable of crushing Flamineo (which Brachiano had failed to do) and bringing swift justice upon the heads of the murderers.

Cornelia and Marcello provide a balance and a contrast to Vittoria and Flamineo, the four making up a family which reflects the chaos and disruption in the State, with the virtuous members apparently weak and helpless in the face of determined and vigorous corruption. Neither Marcello nor Cornelia are fully developed as characters. It is the fact of their virtue, with the contrasts and moral lessons to which this gives rise, that matters; not their individual natures. Nevertheless both parts, but

*T. Bogard: *The Tragic Satire of John Webster*, University of California Press, Berkeley, 1955, p. 60.

Cornelia's in particular, are given typical Websterian energy and some spectacular moments, especially in or just before death. They both have argumentative exchanges with Flamineo, but without effective communication, as he sees Vittoria's adultery in terms of 'preferment' and they describe it as 'ruin' or a 'fall' (see III.1.37–8 and I.2.269). It has been pointed out that despite their claims to virtue they are content to live under Brachiano's roof after his marriage to Vittoria, but their presence there is used by Webster to emphasise the disintegration of Brachiano's court; Marcello's callous murder and Cornelia's subsequent madness envelop the court in a shroud of evil from which it barely emerges at the end of the play.

The language

The White Devil is written mainly in blank verse, a term applied to lines which do not rhyme and contain ten alternately-stressed syllables, e.g.:

> Should for-/tune rend/his sails,/and split/his mast./

> (II.1.107)

This line, which consists of five feet (metrical units) of two syllables each, the first stressed and the second unstressed, is the regular standard line of the play, but Webster continually varies this basic line in order to achieve flexibility and avoid monotony. A number of typical variations can be seen in the following two lines:

> VITTORIA: O my greatest sin lay in my blood.
> Now my blood pays for't.
> FLAMINEO: Th'art a noble sister.

> (V.6.240–1)

These lines are metrically irregular; stressed and unstressed syllables are not where we expect them, with the result that a special emphasis is placed on such a word as 'blood' – a key word in the play, with a combined meaning of life-blood and lust. Neither line is ten syllables long, an irregularity which can help suggest agitation; compare Lodovico's passion after Flamineo has struck him (III.3.128–36). The second line is divided between more than one speaker, a device often used by Webster to increase the speed of conversational flow (see III.1.32–64).

Another variation in the verse is the use of rhyme, and Webster makes a particularly striking use of rhymed couplets. Because the blank verse in *The White Devil* is so irregular, the rhyming couplets draw added attention to themselves, and because they are remote from normal speech they are less personalised than the more individualistic language found elsewhere. They are used by Webster as a vehicle for general comments that often contain moral lessons, like the one which completes the play:

> Let guilty men remember their black deeds
> Do lean on crutches, made of slender reeds.
>
> (V.6.300-1)

Here, as in most scenes in the play, a rhymed couplet gives a neat sense of finality. The frequency of such *sententiae* shows how the language of the play reflects Webster's tendency to move from the particular to the general, to universalise his drama.

Verse is normally a sign of high rank or education and its use generally denotes matters of high seriousness. It is more formal and rhetorical than common language, uses more figures of speech and lends itself to declamation, or 'speechifying'. There is a good deal of the latter in *The White Devil*, for a number of reasons. Firstly, not only are there a number of formal occasions, such as the trial and the wedding celebration, but the characters often behave as if on public show; they *perform* and Webster provides commentators who present them to us. Secondly there is little that is commonplace in the play; it proceeds at a high level of intensity throughout, and characters often speak in very emotional language. Thirdly, this is a play concerned with deceitfulness, and one form of this is for characters to hide their true feelings behind verse rhetoric. Vittoria excels at this in her trial, but is cut short when she tries to deceive her brother with it:

> VITTORIA: I prithee yet remember,
>   Millions are now in graves, which at last day
>   Like mandrakes shall rise shrieking.
> FLAMINEO: Leave your prating,
>   For these are but grammatical laments . . .
>
> (V.6.65-8)

Flamineo explains that Vittoria is concerned only with the form or manner of her speech and not the subject matter. Verse is used similarly throughout the play to conceal rather than communicate thought. The most extreme case of artificiality is its use by the prosecution lawyer at the trial, whose language is practically impenetrable (see III.2.26–50). The finest example of its rhetorical complexity and persuasiveness is Monticelso's speech defining a whore, with its repeated refrain, 'What is a whore?' (see III.2.78–101).

Not all the play is written in verse, although its small prose element is almost entirely limited to one character, Flamineo. Prose has a more natural rhythm. It is more flexible (as befits the most flexible character in the play), being uncontrolled by any rules about metre, syllable-count or rhyme. It lends itself to spontaneous expression in informal situations, and when Flamineo switches from verse to prose it is sometimes to indicate informality or familiarity with his interlocutor. He first talks prose to Brachiano when he wants to get closer to the duke in order to draw him and Vittoria into adultery:

> 'Bove merit! we may now talk freely: 'bove merit; what is't you doubt? her coyness? that's but the superficies of lust most women have; yet why should ladies blush to hear that nam'd, which they do not fear to handle?
>
> (I.2.17–20)

The words 'we may now talk freely' indicate why there has been a change to prose. Flamineo's prose provides most of the light relief from the almost unrelieved intensity of the play. It is generally witty, coarse, and very down-to-earth. Flamineo's constant changing from verse to prose reflects both his mercurial character and his mastery of disguise. He often turns to prose at times when he wishes to distract attention from his true feelings. It is the means of his 'feign'd garb of mirth' (III.1.30) and his 'talk[ing] knave and madman' (IV.2.244). Through Flamineo in particular the play shows that in order to be a master of disguise one must be a master of language. He is just as skilled in verse as in prose and can switch from one to the other even within the same speech (see V.6.107–18 and V.6.148–67), and at one point provides a deflating prose commentary within the lines of some inflated rhyming verse (see IV.2.25–41). By varying the language of *The White Devil* in such ways Webster reinforces the polarisation of points of view which provides the vital contrasts in the play, particularly the gap between what appears to be and what really is, thus matching form and content in a striking and successful way.

Part 4

Hints for study

Approaching the play

Studying a play requires a different approach than you would use for other forms of literature. This is simply because a play is not designed for reading but for live performance on a stage. In order to understand the way in which any play works, you must think in terms of the way in which speeches and situations should be presented on a stage. There are numerous *theatrical* effects, the significance of which can be easily overlooked in studying the text alone. Consider the startling visual impact of the torchlight procession near the start of the play, of the two dumb shows, of the trial scene, the papal election, the marriage procession and, finally, of the tournament at which Brachiano meets his death. All these scenes are primarily *spectacles* and you must try to think of them in visual terms, not least because the surface glitter of the court world, behind which lies extreme corruption, is the means by which Webster most effectively conveys his central idea about the attractiveness of evil. Webster conceived his play in visual terms and, generally speaking, it is actions rather than words, gesture and movement rather than character, that are most memorable – as when Brachiano breaks in upon the trial and demands maximum attention by sitting on his lavishly expensive gown, which he ostentatiously leaves behind him.

The following suggestions will help you to become aware of the theatrical dimension when reading the play:

(i) Make a note of which characters are on stage in each scene and assume that the presence of each character serves some purpose. Try to work out what this might be. Webster composes a picture on the stage and the arrangement can be of significance in itself. Consider Act I Scene 2, in which Flamineo looks on as his sister is prostituted, and Cornelia in turn overlooks the entire scene. This deliberate grouping represents a ruined household.

(ii) Consider in particular how a character might contribute even when silent. For example, an audience will be just as interested in the unspoken response of Vittoria and Zanche as in Flamineo's words when the latter rises from the dead in Act V Scene 6.

(iii) It is worth giving special attention to visual effects referred to in the play, either in speeches or in stage directions, as these are

easily overlooked when reading. Costume, props and set
contribute greatly to the impression a scene makes. Consider, for
example, the implications of the sight of men dressed as holy
friars, bearing 'unction' and 'a crucifix and hallowed candle', and
the contrast this makes with the tormenting and strangling of
Brachiano which they perpetrate. The gap between appearance
and reality is established without words.

(iv) Directors and actors have to decide on the *tone* in which words
must be spoken, and you should also try to determine the correct
tone of voice as you read the play, as you may become more
aware of ambiguities. This can be a crucial matter in a play like
The White Devil in which characters are often ambiguously
presented. One's reaction to Vittoria, for example, depends on
how an actress balances hypocrisy and sincerity, harshness and
softness in her portrayal. How should the line 'How shall's rid
him hence?' (I.2.161) be spoken – in a plaintive or a conspiratorial
tone; by a helpless woman or a would-be murderess?

Do not think of each scene in the play as a self-enclosed unit. Scenes are
interdependent, and you should make a conscious effort to take into
account what has just taken place at the start of a scene and what is
about to happen at its close. This is a particularly rewarding way of
approaching *The White Devil* as Webster juxtaposes contrasting scenes
to give us a different perspective on what we have just witnessed or are
about to witness, often with an ironic effect. Take, for example,
Flamineo's words opening Act V:

> In all the weary minutes of my life,
> Day ne'er broke up till now. This marriage
> Confirms me happy.

These are doubly ironical when the reader considers the previous scene
in which the revenge plot which will take his life was coming to a head,
and the subsequent scene in which the disintegration of the Brachiano
household will begin. Observe which scenes are next to which and try to
think of reasons why they should be placed together.

Make a note of the key images, ones which reappear throughout the
play, and consider what contribution they make to the overall meaning
of the play. For example, the play contains numerous references to
'blood', which can refer to life-blood, family honour, or lust, and is
associated with sin and death throughout the play. Compare Vittoria's
early remark,

> I do protest if any chaste denial,
> If anything but blood could have allayed
> His long suit to me . . .   (I.2.291–3)

with her realisation, spoken at the end as she is dying,

> O my greatest sin lay in my blood.
> Now my blood pays for't.

(V.6.240–1)

This repeated image brings together crime and punishment, lust, murder, and death to reinforce the moral lesson at the heart of the play. As an exercise, extract all the references to devils and witchcraft, and consider whether or not they form a coherent theme.

As essay questions on plays often demand character studies, you should be aware of the main ways in which a dramatist can establish a character:

(i) By what a character says. In a novel the author can tell us directly what a character's personality is and what he is thinking, but the playwright cannot interrupt his play to guide our response to *his* characters. Although we principally judge a character by what he says, we must also take into account when he says it and to whom he is speaking. A character is most likely to reveal his true nature in a soliloquy or an aside, when he has no reason to disguise his true feelings (for example, V.4.113–23 or V.3.170).

(ii) By a character's actions. In a play like *The White Devil* which is full of deception, it is safest to judge characters by what they do rather than what they say. However entertaining is Flamineo in his speech, and however vivacious Vittoria in hers, we must remember that the former murders his brother in cold blood and prostitutes his sister, while the latter is an adulterous accessory to a double murder.

(iii) By what other characters say about him, particularly behind his back. Our attitude to a character is conditioned by the opinion others have of him and this must be measured against what he says or does. A major difficulty in *The White Devil* is that so few of the characters are honest that we distrust their assessments of each other. We may feel that the description of 'whore' which Monticelso applies to Vittoria tells us more about his own lurid imagination than her nature. Such opinions can cause difficult ambiguities, as when Flamineo defames Giovanni, concluding, 'He hath his uncle's villainous look already' (V.4.30), which could, depending on how far we trust Flamineo's commentary, cast doubt on the apparently hopeful ending to the play.

In some plays, particularly Shakespeare's, we look for development in character, but there is little sense in *The White Devil* of any gradual modification of personality as a result of an individual's experiences. A useful exercise is to trace each character through the play to see if there *are* any signs of change. For example, we are told at the start of Act V Scene 6 that Vittoria is carrying a prayer book; does this suggest a development since her first liaison with Brachiano, or is it another example of hypocrisy? In earlier English plays, characters simply represented a single vice or virtue in which they were fixed for the course of the play; is Webster's play close to this kind of drama? Consider to what extent the characters are 'types'; are their reactions predictable; is their behaviour consistent? It is possible to argue that Webster exploits contradictory aspects of character in order to demonstrate that the admirable and the deplorable can coexist? Is there anything in the play to support such a theory? Does Webster deliberately confuse our response to his characters in order to create a world of uncertainty in which no individual's account of himself or another character can be trusted?

Writing an essay

Knowing how to write an essay is as necessary as knowing the text of the play thoroughly. Having achieved the latter, there are a number of common-sense techniques to help you master the former:

(i) Any question demands a reply which is an answer to that question. If you were asked the time of day you would be considered foolish if you described the workings of a clock. In the same way, if an essay question asks you to discuss the relationship between Vittoria and Flamineo, there is no point in referring to, say, the use of the supernatural in the play. The first law of essay writing is *relevance*, absolute relevance which is clear to the examiner. Begin with something like 'There are four main aspects to the relationship between Vittoria and Flamineo', and not with a general comment such as 'London at the turn of the seventeenth century was a rapidly growing city'.

(ii) Avoid repetition; even a summary in the final paragraph is a waste of time and space. The way to avoid repetition is to follow an essay plan which directs you to cover a new point in each paragraph.

(iii) Illustrate each point made with either a relevant quotation from, or close reference to, the text. It is not sufficient to assert, for example, that Flamineo's relationship with his sister is inconsistent. You must support assertions with evidence from the play. In this case you could point to Flamineo's line 'O let me kill her' (V.6.176) in contrast with his attitude to Vittoria a few minutes later, 'Th'art a noble sister – /I'love thee now'

(V.6.241–2). You should also proceed to draw conclusions from your quotation, rather than leaving the examiner to work out its relevance. You could observe, for example, that these quotations reflect both Flamineo's mercurial character and the mixed response that Vittoria's behaviour elicits.

Specimen essay

Discuss the theme of reward and punishment in *The White Devil*.

The White Devil is a study, in dramatic form, of a corrupt court. At the centre of this corruption and hence at the centre of the play is the iniquitous system by which the court functions, luring those dependent on its great wealth with promises of reward, but only punishing with corruption (and possibly violent death) those whose services it has exploited. The theme is stated at the very opening of the play:

> LODOVICO: Banish'd?
> ANTONELLI: It griev'd me much to hear the sentence.
> LODOVICO: Ha, ha, O Democritus thy gods
>   That govern the whole world! – Courtly reward,
>   And punishment!
>
>   (I.1.1–4)

From this point onwards Webster never loses sight of this theme. The structure of the play depends on it; the moral fabric of the play is woven out of it; the ironic tone of the play, centring on the gap between illusion and reality, is a product of it, and all the characters in the play are in some way controlled by it.

The plot is shaped by reward and punishment. All the actions in the play are motivated by either one or the other, one group seeking rewards which directly bring retribution upon their heads from the other group. This becomes clear in the final act of the play when the illusory rewards are replaced by actual Punishment. Having reached the apex of their fortunes (see IV.2.220–1 and V.1.1–3) Brachiano, Vittoria and Flamineo become victims of the court system. Lodovico, the executioner, recalls the opening words of the play:

> Fool! Princes give rewards by their own hands,
> But death or punishment by the hands of others.   (V.6.188–9)

However, even Lodovico falls victim to this perpetual cycle; there is no reward for his service to Francisco, as Giovanni, Brachiano's replacement, deals out swift retribution: 'see my honoured lord,/What use you ought make of their punishment' (V.6.298–9). It is possible to make a structural division in the play between a revenge group and its victims; but a further and more revealing division is between the great men who control the court system of reward and punishment, and the exploited group who seek elusive advancement.

The morality of the characters is conditioned by this system and the moral framework of the play is rooted in it. The play poses the question: what is it that is rewarded in a corrupt court? Marcello chooses virtue and honest service and, as Flamineo scornfully points out, remains unrewarded:

> ... what hast got?
> But like the wealth of captains, a poor handful,
> Which in thy palm thou bears't, as men hold water ... (III.1.41–3)

Neither does Flamineo's learning reap reward, and the lesson he draws is that virtue must be sacrificed and vice embraced to secure prosperity at court:

> ... how shall we find reward?
> But as we seldom find the mistletoe
> Sacred to physic on the builder oak
> Without a mandrake by it, so in our quest of gain.   (III.1.49–52)

The play demonstrates that the court rewards neither honest nor dishonest service, but also that even the great princes who control the court system must submit to a wider 'system' which will ultimately engulf them. Cornelia sums up this larger moral which lies behind the play in her words spoken over the dead body of Marcello:

> His wealth is summ'd, and this is all his store:
> This poor men get; and great men get no more.   (V.4.109–10)

The great irony of the play is that the reality of death is all that lies behind the violent and vicious scramble for rewards. Webster exploits this ironic twist throughout the play, particularly in the fortunes of Flamineo. As he is the character most single-minded in his pursuit of reward so his sacrifices to it are greatest. He gambles his sister, mother, brother and his own life in order to win absolutely nothing. He was 'not a suit the richer' (I.2.327) before prostituting Vittoria to his master and, ironically, he admits to being in exactly the same position as his career of crime draws to its close:

> Why here's an end of all my harvest, he has given me nothing –
> Court promises! Let wise men count them curst ...   (V.3.187–8)

Brachiano's dying description of Flamineo 'dancing on ... ropes' in hell, with 'A money-bag in each hand, to keep him even' (V.3.110–11) is a just summary of his dangerous pursuit of wealth. He is under no illusion about the risks he runs (at one point literally refusing to turn his back on Brachiano), but he is driven inexorably onwards to claim his dividend. Brachiano dead, Flamineo seeks 'Vittoria's bounty', but is only offered the reward of Cain, God's curse (V.6.7–14).

As all the characters in the play are dependent upon the court, so they are all to some extent involved in or affected by the corrupt system of reward and punishment. If not tainted by it, the few good characters are still victims of it. The other victims sacrifice their virtue for rewards, while the great men, with their repeated talk of 'thunder' and 'cannons' (e.g. II.1.60–74) are obsessed with punishment, what Monticelso calls 'Th'bloody audit, and the fatal gripe' (IV.1.19). Flamineo, as we have seen, is central to this theme of reward and punishment, but his sister follows a parallel route, albeit with a less wholehearted commitment. Her manner of speech to Brachiano is similar to Flamineo's:

What have I gain'd by thee but infamy? . . .
Is this your palace? . . .
Who hath the honour to advance Vittoria
To this incontinent college? is't not you?
Is't not your high preferment?   (IV.2.107–18)

Here the hoped-for 'gain' turns to 'infamy' just as Flamineo's 'promises' of reward were revealed as 'curst'. Hence the court itself can be seen as the 'white devil' of the play's title. The rewards which the glittering court offers are indeed 'white', but they prove to be an illusion, behind which trails the punishment of painful death and even damnation.

The above essay is based on the following essay plan:

  (i) Definition of theme – court system
     Centrality of theme: for example, Lodovico
     Main aspects of the play influenced by the theme

  (ii) Influence on structure
     Play moves towards expected reward, plotted punishment: for example, in Act V, downturn of fortunes of Brachiano faction
     Cyclical effect of reward and punishment
     Character grouping can be based on this theme

  (iii) Influence on moral framework
     Moral pressure on those seeking courtly reward
     Neither honest nor dishonest service prospers
     In death a wider moral system is involved

  (iv) Influence on nature of the play – irony in gap between reward and punishment: for example Flamineo (greatest sacrifice, smallest gain)
     Flamineo – no illusions but still pursues reward

(v) Influence on all characters – all part of the system
   Good characters are victims
   Great men obsessed with punishment
   Vittoria's pursuit of gain, parallels Flamineo
   Court is 'white devil' of the play

The points listed above are only a selection from the possible ideas relevant to the topic. For example, there is no discussion of why Francisco evades punishment, and whether or not divine justice or fate are shown to play a part in the scheme of retribution. Points which are less elusive or complex have been discussed as they could be handled reasonably well in a short space. In examinations, when you are short of time, it is necessary to select in this way, just as it is necessary to choose only a few examples to illustrate your points. The entire essay could have been about Flamineo alone, but only at the expense of weakening the main argument which is the centrality of the theme. Although the above essay-plan rightly maps out the separate compartments of the essay, when plans are expanded efforts should be made to link paragraphs so that they merge, in order to prevent a fragmentary effect in your essay.

Essay questions

The following questions are arranged so that the more difficult ones appear lower down the list.

(1) Give an account of the character of either (a) Francisco or (b) Isabella.

(2) Assess the significance of Lodovico's contribution to *The White Devil*.

(3) What do we learn about Vittoria from her conduct during her trial?

(4) Can Brachiano be considered the tragic hero of *The White Devil*?

(5) Discuss the extent to which Flamineo can be considered comic.

(6) 'The focal point of the tragedy is not a character, but a theme, the white devil' (Dallby). Discuss.

(7) 'Webster seems to have conceived the work less as an organic development than a series of set pieces' (Smith). Comment on this view of *The White Devil*.

(8) 'This is more a tragedy of a brother and a sister than a lover and his mistress' (Brennan). Discuss this view of *The White Devil*.

(9) 'Vittoria is dishonourable: Webster simply makes her behave as if she were honourable. This is an artistic insincerity – a lie in the poet's heart' (Jack). Do you agree?

(10) '[An] attempt to shore up chaos with a sententious philosophy' (Jack). Consider the use made of *sententiae* in *The White Devil* in the light of this remark.

Part 5

Suggestions for further reading

The text

The text of *The White Devil* used in these Notes is the Revels edition:
WEBSTER: *The White Devil*, ed. J. Russell Brown, Methuen, London,
  1960; reprinted by Manchester University Press, 1979.
Another edition which is well annotated and has a good introduction is
in the New Mermaids series:
WEBSTER: *The White Devil*, ed. E. M. Brennan, Ernest Benn, London,
  1966.

Other works by Webster

A very useful and inexpensive collection of Webster plays, including *The
Duchess of Malfi* and *The Devil's Law Case* as well as *The White Devil*, is
in the Penguin English Library series:
WEBSTER: *John Webster: Three Plays*, ed. D. C. Gunby, Penguin Books,
  Harmondsworth, 1972.

Critical works

Webster has not been particularly well served by critics, and little
criticism can be wholeheartedly recommended. Some of the best
criticism has appeared in short articles which have been gathered into
useful collections containing a proportion of material relevant to *The
White Devil*.
HOLDSWORTH, R. V. (ED.): *Webster, 'The White Devil' and 'The Duchess of
  Malfi': a Casebook*, Macmillan, London, 1975. Contains selections
  from early as well as modern criticism and some reviews of
  productions; of particular interest are articles by Ian Jack and Roma
  Gill.
HUNTER, G. K. and HUNTER, S. K. (EDS.): *John Webster, a Critical Anthology*,
  Penguin Books, Harmondsworth, 1969. A chronological selection
  from contemporaneous remarks on Webster up to recent scholarship.
  The most vital articles are those by T. S. Eliot, H. T. Price, Inga-Stina
  Ekeblad, and H. Jenkins.

MORRIS, B. (ED.): *John Webster*, Mermaid Critical Commentaries, Ernest Benn, London, 1970. A collection of papers delivered at a symposium in York University. The most valuable are those by A. J. Smith, J. R. Mulryne and Peter Thomson.

There have been a number of book-length studies of Webster:

BERRY, R: *The Art of John Webster*, Clarendon Press, Oxford, 1972. The most useful parts of this book are those which deal with imagery, but the main thesis of the book – that Webster is a baroque artist – appears not worth the space it takes to develop.

BOGARD, T: *The Tragic Satire of John Webster*, University of California Press, Berkeley and Los Angeles, 1955. There are valuable insights throughout this book, but it suffers from unconvincing attempts to make all things in Webster's plays primarily satirical.

BRADBROOK, M. C.: *John Webster: Citizen and Dramatist*, Weidenfeld & Nicolson, London, 1980. This is essential reading. Its strength lies not so much in critical analyses as in its detailed account of Webster's dramatic career and the social, political and literary context in which he lived.

DALLBY, A.: *The Anatomy of Evil: a Study of John Webster's 'The White Devil'*, Lund Studies in English, CWK Gleerup, Lund, 1974. Unlike the last two books this is solely about *The White Devil*. It seeks to establish that the theme of appearance and reality is central to the play, and is a very thorough study, particularly good on Webster's rhetorical techniques and imagery.

GUNBY, D. C.: *Webster: The White Devil*, Edward Arnold, London, 1971. A short study of the play which is mainly a summary of the plot, but does contain a good commentary on Webster's preface to the reader.

LEECH, C.: *John Webster: a Critical Study*, Hogarth Lectures on Literature 16, London, 1951. A very readable attempt at a comprehensive study of the dramatist that has greatly influenced later criticism.

MOORE, D.: *John Webster and his Critics, 1617–1964*. Louisiana State University Press, Baton Rouge, 1966. A digest of trends and developments in criticism of Webster together with some analysis and commentary by the author.

Sources

BOKLUND, G.: *The Sources of 'The White Devil'*, Uppsala University Press, Uppsala, 1957. An exhaustive investigation which traces over a hundred variations of Webster's story. It sheds light on Webster's creative method.

Background

TILLYARD, E. M. W.: *The Elizabethan World Picture*, Chatto & Windus, London, 1943. An elementary account of the orthodox world-view under threat at Webster's time.

BRADBROOK, M. C.: *Themes and Conventions of Elizabethan Tragedy*, Cambridge University Press, Cambridge, 1935. This provides a useful account of Webster's literary context, and contains a section on Webster himself.

ELLIS-FERMOR, U. M.: *The Jacobean Drama: an Interpretation*, revised edition, Methuen, London, 1958. This has a good introduction to Jacobean drama as well as a stimulating chapter on Webster.

GURR, A.: *The Shakespearean Stage, 1574–1642*, Cambridge University Press, 1970. A good general account of theatres, acting companies, actors and stage conditions of Webster's time.

BELSEY, C.: *The Subject of Tragedy: Identity and Difference in Renaissance Drama,* Methuen, London, 1985. Has a stimulating section on *The White Devil.*

DOLLIMORE, J.: *Radical Tragedy: Religion, Ideology and Power in the Drama of Shakespeare and his Contemporaries,* Harvester, Brighton, 1984. This, and Belsey's book above, are good examples of recent, more politically sensitive and critically self-conscious work on the Renaissance period.

The author of these notes

MICHAEL JARDINE is a graduate of the University of Newcastle upon Tyne and the Shakespeare Institute of the University of Birmingham. He was a lecturer in English at Ahmadu Bello University, Nigeria, before becoming a lecturer at King Alfred's College of Higher Education, Winchester, in 1978. He is the editor of the interdisciplinary journal *Contexts and Connections*; has written the York Notes on Shakespeare's *Henry IV Part Two*; and is currently writing a book on literary patronage, the book trade, censorship, and other aspects of the professional writer's milieu. He has also edited Henry Porter's *The Two Angry Women of Abingdon* for the Nottingham Drama Texts series.

York Notes: list of titles

CHINUA ACHEBE
A Man of the People
Arrow of God
Things Fall Apart

EDWARD ALBEE
Who's Afraid of Virginia Woolf?

ELECHI AMADI
The Concubine

ANONYMOUS
Beowulf
Everyman

JOHN ARDEN
Serjeant Musgrave's Dance

AYI KWEI ARMAH
The Beautyful Ones Are Not Yet Born

W. H. AUDEN
Selected Poems

JANE AUSTEN
Emma
Mansfield Park
Northanger Abbey
Persuasion
Pride and Prejudice
Sense and Sensibility

HONORÉ DE BALZAC
Le Père Goriot

SAMUEL BECKETT
Waiting for Godot

SAUL BELLOW
Henderson, The Rain King

ARNOLD BENNETT
Anna of the Five Towns

WILLIAM BLAKE
Songs of Innocence, Songs of Experience

ROBERT BOLT
A Man For All Seasons

ANNE BRONTË
The Tenant of Wildfell Hall

CHARLOTTE BRONTË
Jane Eyre

EMILY BRONTË
Wuthering Heights

ROBERT BROWNING
Men and Women

JOHN BUCHAN
The Thirty-Nine Steps

JOHN BUNYAN
The Pilgrim's Progress

BYRON
Selected Poems

ALBERT CAMUS
L'Etranger (The Outsider)

GEOFFREY CHAUCER
Prologue to the Canterbury Tales
The Franklin's Tale
The Knight's Tale
The Merchant's Tale
The Miller's Tale
The Nun's Priest's Tale
The Pardoner's Tale
The Wife of Bath's Tale
Troilus and Criseyde

ANTON CHEKHOV
The Cherry Orchard

SAMUEL TAYLOR COLERIDGE
Selected Poems

WILKIE COLLINS
The Moonstone
The Woman in White

SIR ARTHUR CONAN DOYLE
The Hound of the Baskervilles

WILLIAM CONGREVE
The Way of the World

JOSEPH CONRAD
Heart of Darkness
Lord Jim
Nostromo
The Secret Agent
Victory
Youth and *Typhoon*

STEPHEN CRANE
The Red Badge of Courage

BRUCE DAWE
Selected Poems

WALTER DE LA MARE
Selected Poems

DANIEL DEFOE
A Journal of the Plague Year
Moll Flanders
Robinson Crusoe

CHARLES DICKENS
A Tale of Two Cities
Bleak House
David Copperfield
Great Expectations
Hard Times
Little Dorrit
Nicholas Nickleby
Oliver Twist
Our Mutual Friend
The Pickwick Papers

EMILY DICKINSON
Selected Poems

JOHN DONNE
Selected Poems

THEODORE DREISER
Sister Carrie

GEORGE ELIOT
Adam Bede
Middlemarch
Silas Marner
The Mill on the Floss

T. S. ELIOT
Four Quartets
Murder in the Cathedral
Selected Poems
The Cocktail Party
The Waste Land

J. G. FARRELL
The Siege of Krishnapur

GEORGE FARQUHAR
The Beaux Stratagem

WILLIAM FAULKNER
Absalom, Absalom!
As I Lay Dying
Go Down, Moses
The Sound and the Fury

HENRY FIELDING
Joseph Andrews
Tom Jones

F. SCOTT FITZGERALD
Tender is the Night
The Great Gatsby

E. M. FORSTER
A Passage to India
Howards End

ATHOL FUGARD
Selected Plays

JOHN GALSWORTHY
Strife

MRS GASKELL
North and South

WILLIAM GOLDING
Lord of the Flies
The Inheritors
The Spire

OLIVER GOLDSMITH
She Stoops to Conquer
The Vicar of Wakefield

ROBERT GRAVES
Goodbye to All That

GRAHAM GREENE
Brighton Rock
The Heart of the Matter
The Power and the Glory

THOMAS HARDY
Far from the Madding Crowd
Jude the Obscure
Selected Poems
Tess of the D'Urbervilles
The Mayor of Casterbridge
The Return of the Native
The Trumpet Major
The Woodlanders
Under the Greenwood Tree

L. P. HARTLEY
The Go-Between
The Shrimp and the Anemone

NATHANIEL HAWTHORNE
The Scarlet Letter

SEAMUS HEANEY
Selected Poems

ERNEST HEMINGWAY
A Farewell to Arms
For Whom the Bell Tolls
The African Stories
The Old Man and the Sea

GEORGE HERBERT
Selected Poems

HERMANN HESSE
Steppenwolf

BARRY HINES
Kes

HOMER
The Iliad

ANTHONY HOPE
The Prisoner of Zenda

GERARD MANLEY HOPKINS
Selected Poems

WILLIAM DEAN HOWELLS
The Rise of Silas Lapham

RICHARD HUGHES
A High Wind in Jamaica

THOMAS HUGHES
Tom Brown's Schooldays

ALDOUS HUXLEY
Brave New World

HENRIK IBSEN
A Doll's House
Ghosts
Hedda Gabler

HENRY JAMES
Daisy Miller
The Europeans
The Portrait of a Lady
The Turn of the Screw
Washington Square

SAMUEL JOHNSON
Rasselas

BEN JONSON
The Alchemist
Volpone

JAMES JOYCE
A Portrait of the Artist as a Young Man
Dubliners

JOHN KEATS
Selected Poems

RUDYARD KIPLING
Kim

D. H. LAWRENCE
Sons and Lovers
The Rainbow
Women in Love

CAMARA LAYE
L'Enfant Noir

HARPER LEE
To Kill a Mocking-Bird

LAURIE LEE
Cider with Rosie

THOMAS MANN
Tonio Kröger

CHRISTOPHER MARLOWE
Doctor Faustus
Edward II

ANDREW MARVELL
Selected Poems

W. SOMERSET MAUGHAM
Of Human Bondage
Selected Short Stories

J. MEADE FALKNER
Moonfleet

HERMAN MELVILLE
Billy Budd
Moby Dick

THOMAS MIDDLETON
Women Beware Women

THOMAS MIDDLETON and WILLIAM ROWLEY
The Changeling

ARTHUR MILLER
Death of a Salesman
The Crucible

JOHN MILTON
Paradise Lost I & II
Paradise Lost IV & IX
Selected Poems

V. S. NAIPAUL
A House for Mr Biswas

SÉAN O'CASEY
Juno and the Paycock
The Shadow of a Gunman

GABRIEL OKARA
The Voice

EUGENE O'NEILL
Mourning Becomes Electra

GEORGE ORWELL
Animal Farm
Nineteen Eighty-four

JOHN OSBORNE
Look Back in Anger

WILFRED OWEN
Selected Poems

ALAN PATON
Cry, The Beloved Country

THOMAS LOVE PEACOCK
Nightmare Abbey and *Crotchet Castle*

HAROLD PINTER
The Birthday Party
The Caretaker

PLATO
The Republic

ALEXANDER POPE
Selected Poems

THOMAS PYNCHON
The Crying of Lot 49

SIR WALTER SCOTT
Ivanhoe
Quentin Durward
The Heart of Midlothian
Waverley

PETER SHAFFER
The Royal Hunt of the Sun

WILLIAM SHAKESPEARE
A Midsummer Night's Dream
Antony and Cleopatra
As You Like It
Coriolanus
Cymbeline
Hamlet
Henry IV Part I
Henry IV Part II
Henry V
Julius Caesar
King Lear
Love's Labour's Lost
Macbeth
Measure for Measure
Much Ado About Nothing
Othello
Richard II
Richard III
Romeo and Juliet
Sonnets
The Merchant of Venice
The Taming of the Shrew
The Tempest
The Winter's Tale
Troilus and Cressida
Twelfth Night
The Two Gentlemen of Verona

GEORGE BERNARD SHAW
Androcles and the Lion
Arms and the Man
Caesar and Cleopatra
Candida
Major Barbara
Pygmalion
Saint Joan
The Devil's Disciple

MARY SHELLEY
Frankenstein

PERCY BYSSHE SHELLEY
Selected Poems

RICHARD BRINSLEY SHERIDAN
The School for Scandal
The Rivals

WOLE SOYINKA
The Lion and the Jewel
The Road
Three Short Plays

EDMUND SPENSER
The Faerie Queene (Book I)

JOHN STEINBECK
Of Mice and Men
The Grapes of Wrath
The Pearl

LAURENCE STERNE
A Sentimental Journey
Tristram Shandy

ROBERT LOUIS STEVENSON
Kidnapped
Treasure Island
Dr Jekyll and Mr Hyde

TOM STOPPARD
Professional Foul
Rosencrantz and Guildenstern are Dead

JONATHAN SWIFT
Gulliver's Travels

JOHN MILLINGTON SYNGE
The Playboy of the Western World

TENNYSON
Selected Poems

W. M. THACKERAY
Vanity Fair

DYLAN THOMAS
Under Milk Wood

EDWARD THOMAS
Selected Poems

FLORA THOMPSON
Lark Rise to Candleford

J. R. R. TOLKIEN
The Hobbit
The Lord of the Rings

CYRIL TOURNEUR
The Revenger's Tragedy

ANTHONY TROLLOPE
Barchester Towers

MARK TWAIN
Huckleberry Finn
Tom Sawyer

VIRGIL
The Aeneid

VOLTAIRE
Candide

EVELYN WAUGH
Decline and Fall
A Handful of Dust

JOHN WEBSTER
The Duchess of Malfi
The White Devil

H. G. WELLS
The History of Mr Polly
The Invisible Man
The War of the Worlds

ARNOLD WESKER
Chips with Everything
Roots

PATRICK WHITE
Voss

OSCAR WILDE
The Importance of Being Earnest

TENNESSEE WILLIAMS
The Glass Menagerie

VIRGINIA WOOLF
To the Lighthouse

WILLIAM WORDSWORTH
Selected Poems

W. B. YEATS
Selected Poems